# SOUTHER OCEAN CRUISING

Sally and Jérôme Poncet

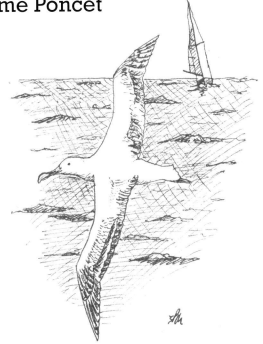

*second edition*

*revised and updated by*
*Sally Poncet, Colin Harris and Susie Grant*

***Southern Ocean Cruising***
First published in the Falkland Islands in 1991 by Sally and Jérôme Poncet.
First Edition © Sally and Jérôme Poncet, 1991. All rights reserved.

Second Edition published in the United Kingdom by Environmental Research & Assessment Ltd, Cambridge, United Kingdom, 2007.
Second Edition © Sally Poncet, Jérôme Poncet, United Kingdom Foreign & Commonwealth Office, and Environmental Research & Assessment Ltd., 2007. All rights reserved.

**ISBN 978-0-9552205-1-7**
**British Library Cataloguing-in-Publication data**
A catalogue record for this publication is available from the British Library.

Citation:   Poncet, S. & Poncet, J. 2007. Southern Ocean Cruising: Second Edition. Revised and updated by S. Poncet, C.M. Harris & S.M. Grant. Environmental Research & Assessment, Cambridge.

Disclaimer
Whilst every care has been taken to ensure the accuracy of the information in this publication, no warranty is given as to its correctness, nor of any advice given, nor responsibility taken for any omissions from the handbook. We hope the publication will be found helpful, but it does not obviate the need for users to make further enquiries as appropriate.

Cover photograph
*Damien II* in King George VI Sound, Antarctic Peninsula, January 1989. © Ben Osborne.

Title page illustration
Albatross, Southern Ocean. © Ellen MacArthur 2007.

Cover design (1st Edition)
Philippe Bertrand & Benoit Heimermann

Maps (2nd Edition)
ERA and Sally Poncet

Layout design (2nd Edition)
Helen de Mattos

Printed and bound in the UK by The Panda Group, Haverhill, Suffolk.
Printed on Take 2 Silk paper (75% recycled with 25% virgin fibre from sustainable sources; ISO14001 certified mill; FSC Certified, NAPM Accredited).

Environmental Research & Assessment Ltd.
Cambridge, United Kingdom
www.era.gs

# Contents

List of maps 6
Note on the maps 8
Map legend 9

Preface to the second edition 11
Acknowledgements 12

1991 Authors' preface 13

Introduction 17

The Antarctic Region 19
Essential documents 19
Protocol on Environmental Protection to the Antarctic Treaty 19
Antarctic Treaty Recommendation XVIII-I 19
Antarctic Treaty Visitor Site Guidelines 20
IAATO Codes of Conduct for Visitors 20
Antarctic Permits, Advance Notice and Post-Visit Reports 20
Environmental impact assessments 21
Safe operations 22
Equipping yourself and your boat 22
Waste disposal 23
Marine pollution 23
Emergency situations 24
Use of vehicles and engines 24
Light pollution 25
Planning site visits and landings 25
Environmental guidelines for landings 27
Birds 27
Seals 28
Plants 28
Geological features 28
Preventing the introduction of non-native species 28
Facilities and structures 30
Rock cairns and depots 30

Historic buildings and unoccupied stations 30
Occupied stations 31
Scientific equipment and instrumentation 32
Site management 32
Antarctic Treaty Visitor Site Guidelines 34
Paulet Island 34
Brown Bluff 36
Snow Hill, Nordenskjöld Hut 38
Turret Point on King George Island 40
Penguin Island 42
Barrientos Island in the Aitcho Islands 45
Yankee Harbour at Greenwich Island 47
Hannah Point on Livingston Island 49
Neko Harbour 51
Cuverville Island 52
Goudier Island and Port Lockroy 'Base A' 54
Jougla Point on Wiencke Island 57
Pléneau Island 58
Petermann Island 60
Antarctic Specially Managed Areas 62
South Shetland Islands 62
Antarctic Peninsula 65
East Antarctica 67
The Ross Sea region 69
Antarctic Specially Protected Areas 71
South Orkney Islands 71
South Shetland Islands 72
Antarctic Peninsula 77
West Antarctica (from 45°E –0°E) 80
East Antarctica (from 0°E – 155°E) 80
The Ross Sea region 82

Southern Ocean Islands North of 60°S 86
Tierra del Fuego 86
South Atlantic islands 90
The Falkland Islands 90
South Georgia 95
South Sandwich Islands 98
Gough Island 98

Bouvetøya                                                              99
South African sub-Antarctic islands                                    99
  Prince Edward Islands                                                99
French sub-Antarctic islands                                          100
  Île Amsterdam                                                       100
  Île Saint-Paul                                                      101
  Îles Crozet                                                         102
  Îles Kerguelen                                                      103
Australian sub-Antarctic islands                                      105
  Heard Island                                                        106
  McDonald Islands                                                    106
  Macquarie Island                                                    107
New Zealand's sub-Antarctic islands                                   108
  Campbell Island                                                     109
  Auckland Islands                                                    110
  Antipodes Islands and Bounty Islands                                110
  Snares Islands                                                      110

**Annex I:**   Guidance for Visitors to the Antarctic                 112
**Annex II:**  Guidance for those Organising and Conducting Tourism
               and Non-governmental Activities in the Antarctic       114
**Annex III:** Marine Wildlife Watching Guidelines                    118
**Annex IV:**  Boot, Clothing and Equipment Decontamination Guidelines
               for Small Boat Operations                              123
**Annex V:**   List of sites within the Antarctic Treaty area where special
               management conditions apply                            126
**Annex VI:**  Historic Sites and Monuments within the Antarctic Treaty area  130
**Annex VII:** Information resources                                  136
**Annex VIII:** Yacht voyages to the Southern Ocean                   142

**Acronyms and abbreviations**                                        160

# List of maps

**Map 1.** The Southern Ocean and Antarctica   17

**Map 2.** The Antarctic Peninsula: permanent stations and sites where Antarctic Treaty Visitor Site Guidelines apply   26

**Map 3.** The South Shetland Islands: permanent stations, sites where Antarctic Treaty Visitor Site Guidelines apply, and Antarctic Specially Managed Areas   33

**Map 4.** Paulet Island, Erebus and Terror Gulf   35

**Map 5.** Brown Bluff, Antarctic Sound   37

**Map 6.** Nordenskjöld Hut, Snow Hill Island   39

**Map 7.** Turret Point, King George Island   41

**Map 8.** Penguin Island   43

**Map 9.** Barrientos Island, Aitcho Islands   45

**Map 10.** Yankee Harbour, Greenwich Island   47

**Map 11.** Hannah Point, Livingston Island   49

**Map 12.** Neko Harbour, Andvord Bay   51

**Map 13.** Cuverville Island, Errera Channel   53

**Map 14.** Goudier Island, Port Lockroy   55

**Map 15.** Jougla Point, Wiencke Island   57

**Map 16.** Pléneau Island   59

**Map 17.** Petermann Island, Penola Strait   61

**Map 18.** Admiralty Bay, ASMA No. 1, King George Island   63

**Map 19.** Deception Island, ASMA No. 4   64

**Map 20.** Palmer Station (US), Arthur Harbour, Anvers Island   65

**Map 21.** East Antarctica: permanent stations, specially managed and protected areas   66

**Map 22.** Cape Denison, ASMA No. 3, Commonwealth Bay   67

**Map 23.** Larsemann Hills, ASMA No. 6, Prydz Bay   69

**Map 24.** The Ross Sea region: permanent stations and protected areas   70

**Map 25.** The McMurdo Dry Valleys, Ross Island and protected areas   71

**Map 26.** The South Orkney Islands: permanent stations and protected areas   72

**Map 27.** Southern Powell Island   72

**Map 28.** The South Shetland Islands: permanent stations and protected areas   73

**Map 29.** Maxwell Bay, King George Island: permanent stations and protected areas   73

**Map 30.** Harmony Point, Nelson Island   74

**Map 31.** English Strait area    74
**Map 32.** Cape Shirreff, Livingston Island    75
**Map 33.** Byers Peninsula, Livingston Island    75
**Map 34.** Western Bransfield Strait    75
**Map 35.** The Antarctic Peninsula: permanent stations and protected areas    76
**Map 36.** Mount Flora, Hope Bay    77
**Map 37.** Cierva Point    77
**Map 38.** Doumer Island    78
**Map 39.** Biscoe Point, Anvers Island    78
**Map 40.** Green Island, Berthelot Islands    79
**Map 41.** Rothera Point, Adelaide Island    79
**Map 42.** Avian Island, Marguerite Bay    79
**Map 43.** Lagotellerie Island, Marguerite Bay    79
**Map 44.** Taylor Rookery and Rookery  Islands    80
**Map 45.** Scullin and Murray Monoliths    81
**Map 46.** Marine Plain and Hawker Island    81
**Map 47.** Haswell Island    82
**Map 48.** Ardery Island and Odbert Island, Northeastern Bailey Peninsula,
             Clark Peninsula, and Frazier Islands    82
**Map 49.** Pointe-Géologie Archipelago    83
**Map 50.** Sabrina Island, Balleny Islands    83
**Map 51.** Cape Hallett    83
**Map 52.** Mt Melbourne and Edmonson Point    84
**Map 53.** Terra Nova Bay    84
**Map 54.** Tierra del Fuego: main settlements and protected areas    87
**Map 55.** The Falkland Islands: main settlements and National Nature Reserves    91
**Map 56.** South Georgia: permanent stations and protected areas.    96
**Map 57.** Marion Island    99
**Map 58.** Prince Edward Island    100
**Map 59.** Île Amsterdam    101
**Map 60.** Île Saint-Paul    101
**Map 61.** Îles Crozet    102
**Map 62.** Île de la Possession    103
**Map 63.** Îles Kerguelen    103
**Map 64.** Golfe du Morbihan, Îles Kerguelen    104
**Map 65.** Heard Island and McDonald Islands    106
**Map 66.** Macquarie Island    107
**Map 67.** Campbell Island    109
**Map 68.** Auckland Islands    110

# Note on the maps

A variety of source data have been used to compile the maps in this edition of the handbook. These data vary in the accuracy of identification of features and locations. Whilst substantial effort has been made to verify the correctness of the maps, it has not been possible to undertake a comprehensive check on accuracy, and we have relied on the best and most up-to-date information available. For these reasons, no warranty can be made about the accuracy or completeness of map content and no liability arising from their use can be accepted. They are intended as a general guide to assist users to locate features described in the text, rather than to provide definitive surveys.

Users should be aware that GPS coordinates are likely to differ from coordinates given on maps owing to the variable accuracy of source data. There may also be conflicting information between map sources because of variations in the age, scale and accuracy of source data.

Most of the maps have been prepared using a Geographic Information System. Maps for the region south of 60°S were largely developed using data from the Antarctic Digital Database (ADD) (v. 4.1), permission for the use of which was kindly granted by the Scientific Committee on Antarctic Research (SCAR). This database is the most comprehensive compilation of digital topographic data available for the Antarctic at scales of approximately 1:250,000 and smaller. The British Antarctic Survey (BAS) coordinates ADD updates on behalf of SCAR, incorporating changes such as ice margin recession, improving feature accuracy as time and resources allow. The ADD holds data that allowed us to distinguish ice-free from ice-covered areas in maps. However, for the sub-Antarctic islands north of 60°S, available data did not allow for such a distinction, and for this reason ice-covered areas are not differentiated and all land areas are shown as white on these maps.

Human features such as stations and protected areas have been compiled by Environmental Research & Assessment (ERA) from recent records held by the Antarctic Treaty Secretariat and from the Council of Managers of National Antarctic Programs (COMNAP), as well as from map data ERA has compiled for specific national programmes. The US National Geophysical Data Center World Vector Shoreline (2006) was used for most coastlines north of 60°S.

**Specific sources and acknowledgements for maps / spatial data are as follows:**

Map 1: ESRI Data and Maps (2003) and ADD (v4.1, 2005).

Maps 4-17: kindly supplied by the Antarctic Treaty Secretariat.

Map 19: based on maps originally prepared by BAS for the Deception Island management plan.

Map 20: based on data compiled by ERA for the United States Antarctic Program.

Maps 22, 48, 65 and 66: data kindly supplied by the Australian Antarctic Division.

Map 41: kindly supplied by BAS.

Maps 52 and 53: protected area data compiled by ERA for the Italian National Antarctic Program.

Map 54: protected area data from UNEP-WCMC / IUCN World Database on Protected Areas (2006).

Map 55: data kindly supplied by Environmental Planning Department, Falkland Islands Government.

Map 56: South Georgia coastal outline and contours kindly supplied by BAS.

Maps 59–64: information on protected areas kindly supplied by Terres Australes et Antarctiques Françaises.

Maps 67 and 68: data kindly supplied by the New Zealand Department of Conservation.

**Map legend**

| | | |
|---|---|---|
| ☐ Permanent ice | ■ Station (year-round) | ▲ Antarctic Treaty Visitor Site Guidelines |
| ▨ Ice-free area | ◪ Station (summer only) | ● Protected area |
| Ocean | ◆ Field hut | ☐ Protected area |
| ⟋ Coastline | ⚓ Preferred anchorage | ⌐ ⌐ Antarctic Specially Managed Area |

*Notes*

Maps 4-17, 19 and 41 have been incorporated with minimal change from the originals, and therefore retain their own system of symbols to represent features.

Maps portraying areas north of 60°S do not differentiate between ice-free and permanently ice-covered areas, and land areas are shown as white on these maps.

# Preface to the second edition

Yachts and cruise ships, scientists and support personnel, we have all contributed to the opening up of Antarctica. With the growing number of visitors, the need to protect the environment is more important than ever. The aim of this *Southern Ocean Cruising* handbook is to provide information to visitors – and to the yachting community in particular – about environmental DOs and DON'Ts that currently apply to the Antarctic region and Southern Ocean islands. The various conservation measures that apply, contact addresses and where to find further information are also provided to assist planning your trip South.

The Southern Ocean is a general term that has long been in use by mariners to describe the seas that extend from the Antarctic continent north to about 40°S. The precise location of this northern boundary is really a matter of personal preference – it may be the Antarctic Treaty boundary at 60°S, or the Polar Front (Antarctic Convergence), or further north still. The area and islands covered in this handbook are principally those of the Antarctic and sub-Antarctic region, and also some more northerly islands and archipelagos that are regularly visited by yachts during their cruise South.

This edition of the original 1991 *Southern Ocean Cruising* handbook has been prepared at the request of the Polar Regions Unit in the Overseas Territories Directorate of the United Kingdom's Foreign and Commonwealth Office. In the 16 years since the first edition appeared, there have been numerous and far-reaching changes to the environmental regulations that govern visits to the Antarctic and sub-Antarctic regions. These include the adoption of the Protocol on Environmental Protection to the Antarctic Treaty (the Protocol) in 1991 by all Antarctic Treaty Consultative Parties, followed in 1994 by the adoption of Recommendation XVIII-1 (*Guidance for Visitors to the Antarctic*), the introduction of new protected areas, and ratification of the Protocol in 1998 with the requirement by some countries for their citizens to obtain a permit from their relevant national authorities before visiting the Antarctic.

The handbook's original text has been comprehensively revised and updated in this new edition, and new maps have been designed in a Geographical Information System based on data kindly supplied by a wide range of experts and organisations (see Note on maps and Acknowledgements). Owing to production costs, only a limited print-run of this edition has been possible. However, in an effort to ensure that all those planning a cruise to the Southern Ocean can gain access to the information, an electronic version is available for download from the website www.era.gs/resources/soc.

## Acknowledgements

Numerous individuals and organisations have been exceptionally helpful in the preparation of this handbook. We are particularly grateful to the Polar Regions Unit, UK Foreign & Commonwealth Office for generous financial support for the preparation of this second edition of *Southern Ocean Cruising*. We wish to thank the Antarctic Treaty Secretariat, Australian Antarctic Division, British Antarctic Survey, Falkland Islands Government, New Zealand Department of Conservation, and the Scientific Committee on Antarctic Research for kindly providing access to digital data used in the production of the maps. The Antarctic Treaty Secretariat also kindly provided the full text of the Antarctic Treaty Visitor Site Guidelines for reproduction in *Southern Ocean Cruising*. We are very grateful to the International Association of Antarctica Tour Operators for providing the full text of the environmental guidelines developed and used by their members.

In addition, we would like to thank the following individuals for their helpful contributions and for comments on the text: Ben Osborne (Cover photo); Ellen MacArthur (Title page sketch); Jérôme Poncet, SV *Golden Fleece*; Marie-Paul Guillaumot, SV *Le Sourire*; Skip Novak, Pelagic Expeditions; Jose Maria Acero and Pablo Wainschenker, Antarctic Treaty Secretariat; Kim Crosbie, Denise Landau, and John Splettstoesser, International Association of Antarctica Tour Operators; Rob Bowman, Joan Harris, Mike Richardson, Stephen Ross, Jane Rumble, and Shirley Williams, Polar Regions Unit, Foreign & Commonwealth Office; Noel Carmichael and Terry Reid, Parks and Wildlife Service of Tasmania; Ewan McIvor, Australian Antarctic Division; Dominique Giudicelli (former Environmental Planning Officer), Helen Otley (Environment Officer), and Robert King (Customs and Immigration Officer), Falkland Islands Government; Christophe Barbraud, Laboratoire de Chize, CNRS, France; Julie Maillot, Cédric Marteau, and Emmanuel Reuillard, Terres Australes et Antarctiques Françaises, France; Pete McClelland, Department of Conservation, New Zealand; Adrian Fox and Peter Fretwell, British Antarctic Survey; Colin Summerhayes, Scientific Committee on Antarctic Research; Polly Penhale, US National Science Foundation; and Fiona Danks, Environmental Research & Assessment.

# 1991 Authors' preface

The Southern Ocean – that vast expanse of water encircling the Antarctic – is a challenging environment where gale-force winds and huge seas can mean exhilaration, and sometimes despair, to those who venture South in small vessels. The region also offers isolation and beauty, and Antarctica and its fringe of sub-Antarctic islands are welcome landfalls to the sailor.

Our personal experience of this environment dates back to 1971, when Jérôme and friend Gérard Janichon aboard their yacht *Damien* sailed to South Georgia, and later Crozet, Kerguelen, Heard and Macquarie islands, the South Shetland Islands and the Antarctic Peninsula. In 1977, Jérôme and I visited South Georgia on *Damien II*, followed by a winter on the Antarctic Peninsula: this was the beginning of our involvement with the Antarctic. Since that 1978 winter we have returned often, accompanied by our three sons, conducting research and exploring the Antarctic region. Based in the Falkland Islands, *Damien II* now spends each summer South, either sailing for pleasure while continuing research on seabird distribution, or on charter to scientific and film crews.

During these years of cruising and working in the Antarctic, we have been increasingly concerned at the lack of information readily available to visitors, particularly yacht crews and private expeditions to the Antarctic. Informing people about the Antarctic environment, its wildlife, the way in which bases operate, and above all advising them how to avoid damaging this beautiful but fragile region are essential steps towards protecting the Antarctic.

Visitors – whether they are tourists, ships' crews, base personnel, or a yacht's complement – are not always a threat to Antarctica's wildlife or ecology, providing they are adequately informed about the environment and how to minimise their impact upon it when passing through.

We can only hope that the Antarctic will remain a continent with no political barriers; a place that the ordinary individual still has the right to see and experience; where all people, be they tourists, sailors, scientists or administrators will continue to safeguard its wilderness. This handbook has been prepared with these hopes in mind.

I recognise that for some, the handbook may come as a disappointment: there are no sailing instructions here, no anchorage descriptions, no handy hints on where to shop or change your dollars. I leave that kind of book to someone else, to a future time. But the day that book is written will signal the end of the Antarctic as a true wilderness area, the end of voyages of exploration and discovery. For the moment, this handbook may ease the current transition from past to future: how successful that transition is, will depend on you.

*Sally*

I hate rules and regulations. I hate manuals and instructions. I hate anything that affects my freedom of choice, my dreams, my spirit of adventure. Why then, have I spent this past year helping Sally prepare a handbook that could be regarded as nothing but an avalanche of interdictions and restrictions?

That I *have* done, still surprises me: I, who twenty five years ago, chose ocean cruising as a way of life, an alternative to the suffocation of Europe, a means of satisfying my need for discovery and open spaces, of avoiding policed regulations. If I was to write about the polar regions, I'd rather describe the beauty of the ice, of certain anchorages now 'out of bounds', or a recipe for seal liver pâté.

So today, if I find myself co-author of this handbook, it's because certain things have changed in me, and on our planet. There are more yachts in the Southern Ocean than ever before, and inevitably adventure and discovery no longer exist in their original form. Nonetheless, the far South – with its unearthly lights, fabulous scenery, its unique ecosystem, and a power that humbles – still exists.

In this privileged realm, constraints upon the visitor are few: there is no money, no visa, no time limit; there are no Customs, Immigration, no formalities; there is no police, no army, no judge. In fact, it is a world in stark and total contrast to all other sailing grounds. We must learn to live here, not as heroes, not as conquerors, profiteers, thieves, not as desecrators, assassins.

As always, it's easy to know what NOT to do, and that's what this handbook is about. What you CAN do and how you do it, is not so easy to explain: your conscience and your intelligence should guide you better than any handbook. One thing is certain though:

a caring attitude will not only protect the Southern Ocean environment and the animals that live there, but it will also safeguard the privileges awaiting future generations of yachts and expeditions who will dream and plan of sailing South: it is your attitude and behaviour now that may determine whether they will be able to or not.

*Post script, May 2006:* So, that was written 15 years ago; for my part, nothing has changed in my feeling for the place and the attitude about it. But the Antarctic is no longer a place of 'administrative freedom', as you will realise when reading this new edition. Now you do need a permit, you do have to provide a mass of information, you are subject to fines and imprisonment in your own country if you break the law. Antarctica has become a place with the most stringent environmental protection rules on Earth. It is still a beautiful place, and these rules were originally made to keep it this way.

In the last 15 years remarkably few yachts have asked for assistance in the Antarctic, neither more nor less than for any other type of logistical operation there. A few required assistance because of bad preparation, a few because of bad luck, but the great majority have been self-sufficient and achieved one of the most powerful cruises of their life.

The message to the yachting community is still the same, possibly even stronger now with the existence of this huge collection of rules: don't make the word 'yacht' become synonymous with 'nuisance'.

*Jérôme*

# Introduction

The first cruising yacht to visit Antarctica was Bill Tilman's *Mischief* in 1966-67, when she called at the South Shetland. However, it was not until the mid-1970s, after the 1972-73 visits of *Damien* and *Icebird*, that yachts began to regularly visit southern waters, no doubt lured by the widely-read accounts of these forerunners of Antarctic cruising. Initially, only one or two yachts each season ventured South, increasing from a half dozen or so in the early 1980s, to over 20 in the 1990-91

**Map 1. The Southern Ocean and Antarctica**

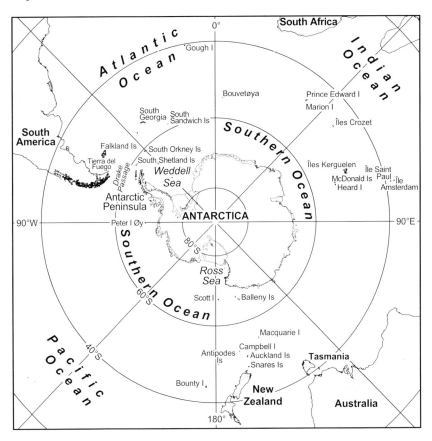

season and the beginning of commercial yacht charter voyages. In 2005-06 there were nearly 30 yacht visits, of which over half were charter voyages.

Yacht visits have caused concern among Antarctic Treaty nations for many years, reflected in such statements as *"The proliferation of private yachts in the Southern Ocean has added a new and largely unwelcome element to the tourist problem. The activities of these yachts seem at the moment, to be beyond any general control."* (Bonner W. and Walton D. 1984. *Antarctica.* Pergamon Press). Tourism in general has been seen by some to be an undesirable activity, a source of disturbance to the Antarctic environment and disruption to the scientific community. In an effort to minimise visitor impacts, comprehensive international regulations were introduced to ensure that all human activities, including scientific research and associated logistical support operations as well as tourism, do not have adverse impacts on the Antarctic environment. Some scientific stations now have strict limits on the number of tourist visits, and site-specific guidelines apply for cruise ship landings at the most popular visitor sites.

The Southern Ocean and all land south of 60°S are governed under provisions agreed in the Antarctic Treaty system. Islands north of 60°S come under the jurisdiction of their respective national governments, and the laws that concern you as a visitor will vary accordingly. However, Antarctic environmental guidelines are just as relevant there as they are further south, and at any remote place where you should do the utmost to ensure that your visit causes as little disturbance as possible. Note that additional or even more stringent conditions may apply at some Southern Ocean islands and that the relevant government agency(ies) should be contacted well before departure to confirm specific requirements.

# The Antarctic Region

## Essential documents

The Antarctic Treaty of 1961, which applies to the area south of 60°S (Map 1), established Antarctica as a zone for peace and science. The continent was designated a Special Conservation Area in 1964 and over the years, special environmental measures have been introduced to help preserve its important values.

In 1991 these measures were rationalised through the adoption of the Protocol on Environmental Protection to the Antarctic Treaty (referred to as the Protocol), which now forms the legal basis for comprehensive protection of the Antarctic environment. The Protocol applies to all activities: tourism, non-governmental and governmental. Visitors are also bound by applicable national laws and regulations according to their country of origin. The following section describes some of the essential documents that you will need to be aware of when planning your visit.

### Protocol on Environmental Protection to the Antarctic Treaty

The Protocol comprises a statement of environmental principles that apply within the Antarctic, three of the most important to note here being:

- activities in the Antarctic Treaty area need to be planned and conducted so as to limit their adverse impacts on the Antarctic environment;
- all activities need to be assessed for their potential environmental impacts before they can be carried out; and
- priority is given to scientific research and the preservation of the value of Antarctica for science.

There are six detailed annexes to the Protocol covering a range of environmental measures:

- Environmental Impact Assessment (Annex I)
- Conservation of Antarctic Fauna and Flora (Annex II)
- Waste Disposal and Waste Management (Annex III)
- Prevention of Marine Pollution (Annex IV)
- Area Protection and Management (Annex V)
- Liability Arising from Environmental Emergencies (Annex VI)

The Protocol and its annexes may be obtained from the Antarctic Treaty Secretariat (www.ats.aq).

### Antarctic Treaty Recommendation XVIII-I

To help ensure that visitors are aware of and are therefore able to comply with the requirements of the Treaty agreements and notably the Protocol, a key document (known as Recommendation XVIII-I)

covering tourism and non-governmental activities was adopted by the Treaty Parties in 1994. It has two main parts:
- *Guidance for Visitors to the Antarctic* – containing information for visitors to help them minimise their impact on the Antarctic environment and its wildlife (see p. 112).
- *Guidance for those Organising and Conducting Tourism and Non-governmental Activities in the Antarctic* – (see p. 114).

Every group organiser, every yacht skipper and every tour operator planning to visit the Antarctic should refer to this document.

### Antarctic Treaty Visitor Site Guidelines

Site-specific information and practical guidance on how landings should be conducted at selected sites are being developed by the Antarctic Treaty Parties in partnership with the cruise ship industry (under the auspices of the International Association of Antarctica Tour Operators (IAATO)) and the scientific research community. At present, such guidelines have been adopted for a number of sites on the South Shetland Islands and Antarctic Peninsula (see p. 34). They can also be obtained from www.ats.aq under 'Topics' > 'Other'.

### International Association of Antarctica Tour Operators Codes of Conduct for Visitors

Environmental protection documents have been developed and adopted by the International Association of Antarctica Tour Operators (IAATO) and provide a comprehensive set of best-practice guidelines for Antarctic tourism (see p. 118 and www.iaato.org). They are used in all wildlife-rich and remote areas visited by IAATO members, which today includes over 30 cruise ship operators and nine charter yachts. We recommend that all yachts visiting the Antarctic and sub-Antarctic regions carry IAATO guidelines on board, and in particular the *IAATO Marine Wildlife Watching Guidelines*. Additionally, IAATO produces a package of information for one-off private yacht expeditions to the Antarctic, updated annually and as each season progresses and available for a fee on request to IAATO.

### Antarctic Permits, Advance Notice and Post-Visit Reports

Before departing for the Antarctic, you are likely to be required to apply for permission to visit (note that an application for a permit is called 'prior notification' and 'Advance Notice' in the document *Guidance for those Organising and Conducting Tourism and Non-governmental Activities in the Antarctic*). Most Antarctic Treaty countries will have domestic legislation setting out the requirements for those wanting to visit Antarctica. These requirements differ from country to country. Some authorities operate a 'permitting system' where you apply for permission to undertake a visit; others require submission of an 'Environmental Impact Assessment for approval'. It is your responsibility to check with your own national authorities about what you need to do in advance of your trip – they will be happy to help you understand their requirements. You should aim to start this process at least 6 months before your intended departure. A useful guide to the different requirements of each country can be found in *Polar Updates* (Rootes and Pasteur, 2006). Contact details for those countries from which most visitors originate (USA, United Kingdom, Germany, France, Australia, New Zealand, Canada, The Netherlands, Belgium, Italy, Spain, Chile and Argentina) are listed in Annex VII (see p. 139).

The skipper, group organiser, tour operator or the person named on the Antarctic Permit is responsible for all areas of permissions, safe operations, environmental emergencies (e.g. oil spills), self-sufficiency and management of people while ashore as well as on board. This person is required to provide passengers and crew with a copy of the *Guidance for Visitors to the Antarctic*, and to ensure that everyone on board is aware of the location of Antarctic Specially Protected Areas (ASPAs), Antarctic Specially Managed Areas (ASMAs), Historic Sites and Monuments (HSMs), and those sites where Antarctic Treaty Visitor Site Guidelines apply, and of the restrictions that apply to these areas.

These regulations effectively mean that anyone organising a cruise to the Antarctic – yacht skipper, expedition organiser, tour operator – will need to apply to their government for an Antarctic permit.

Organisers should provide relevant information to the appropriate national authority in the format requested. Permits and sometimes visas may also be required for Southern Ocean island visits, depending on national legislation – see relevant sections below for details. Some countries may require that you take out third party liability insurance and these details should be included in the application form.

Once your Antarctic visit is over, you must submit a Post-Visit Report about your activities to your national authority (i.e. the authority that granted your permit) within three months of your visit. This report should include the name, details and state of registration of your yacht, the name of skipper, itinerary, the number of visitors engaged in the activities, landing sites, dates and purpose of landings and the number of visitors landed on each occasion. Electronic Post-Visit Report forms can be downloaded from www.iaato.org or www.ats.aq.

**Environmental impact assessments**
The Protocol requires that environmental protection must be a fundamental consideration when planning activities in Antarctica. This effectively means that all proposed activities need to be assessed for their potential impacts before they are carried out. A preliminary assessment is carried out first, to determine whether the activity proposed is likely to cause any environmental impact. In order to complete this preliminary assessment,

you will need to include in your permit application / advance notification form details of any potential environmental impacts that your visit might create. You may also be required to describe how you intend to minimise your impacts.

Full-scale Environmental Impact Assessments (EIAs) (called 'Initial' and 'Comprehensive' Environmental Evaluations in the Protocol) are required if your intended activity is likely to create a significant impact on the environment. For example, a full EIA would typically be required for construction of permanent facilities, or for multi-year activities at a given site. For yacht cruises, impacts are generally of a more minor or transitory nature, and EIAs are usually not required. Your national authority will be able to provide more advice.

## Safe operations

### Equipping yourself and your boat

The Antarctic and Southern Ocean region is probably the most demanding of all sailing environments. Generally it is those who respect and recognise the possible difficulties ahead and prepare themselves, their crew and their yacht accordingly, who will give and get the most enjoyment out of a season down South.

The fundamental requirement of any Southern Ocean cruise is self-sufficiency. Above all else, make sure that you and your yacht are as well prepared and equipped as possible. There are no repair facilities down South. Do not expect

assistance from scientific stations. Make sure that you carry enough spares of all sorts to enable repairs and maintenance to be carried out aboard by you during your voyage. And be prepared for the worst that the Southern Ocean can offer, since no matter how short your crossing to Antarctica may be, there is always the possibility of a knock-down, of dismasting, of injury and worse.

Basic advantages to any polar cruise are a strong-hulled boat – steel or aluminium being the best adapted for Antarctic conditions – sturdy rigging, a powerful engine and large fuel-carrying capacity, a cabin heater, depth sounder, heavy-duty anchor and chain, and extra mooring gear (i.e. spare anchors and chain, mooring lines and anchoring points for lines ashore) plus lots of spares for everything.

There is little likelihood of getting frozen-in inadvertently during a summer trip if you pay attention to weather and avoid extensive fields of pack-ice. Even so, it is a good idea to carry ample supplies of food, particularly if you plan to visit areas where pack-ice could delay you longer than intended. Food, fuel and water are not retailed at any station, and self-sufficiency is the rule for all expeditions, whether private or governmental, and all tourists, whether organised or independent. Take on sufficient fuel for your trip before departure, remembering that there will be many times when you will be motoring, not sailing: winds are often too light, too strong or from the wrong direction, to be relied upon as your only means of propulsion. Remember also to include fuel for the cabin heater when calculating estimated consumption. Freshwater is always available in the form of glacier ice or meltwater.

### Waste disposal

The problem of waste disposal concerns all visitors to the Antarctic, from the largest station to the smallest yacht. There are strict regulations in place on board all vessels and at all stations to ensure that the following measures of waste disposal are observed. All are based on the principle that *'if you can carry it in, you can carry it out'*. Note that waste disposal measures at some sub-Antarctic islands may differ. Whatever method, responsible and effective waste disposal involves planning, organisation and a commitment to protect a unique environment. Garbage compactors and grey-water holding tanks for large yachts are the ideal solution and will help to ensure that the next visitor – and that may still be you – enjoys the beauty of a pristine anchorage.

It is prohibited to dispose of any wastes, including sewage and domestic liquid wastes, onto land or into freshwater streams or lakes. All plastics, glass, wood, metals (including tin cans and fuel drums), ropes, sail cloth, rubber wastes, fuels or used engine / lubricating oils, batteries or battery acid, paper products, dunnage and packing materials must be stored on board until adequate means of disposal on land, outside of the Antarctic Treaty area,

are at hand. Note that all open burning of wastes is prohibited. If you plan to burn wastes you are required to have a closed incinerator that reduces emissions to the minimum practicable, and all incineration residues are required to be removed from the Treaty area.

All residues of carcasses of imported animals and avian products (e.g. chicken bones, eggs) must be removed from the Antarctic Treaty area unless sterilised (e.g. by autoclave or high-temperature incineration). The disposal of all other biodegradable food and sewage should take place not less than 12 nautical miles from the nearest land or ice-shelf. Food wastes should be macerated to a size that can be passed through a 25 mm screen. Sewage should be discharged at a moderate rate, preferably while the vessel is moving at a speed of no less than 4 knots. This applies to all vessels certified to carry more than 10 persons. Yachts carrying 10 persons or less may dispose of sewage closer inshore, but preferably in deep water and with an offshore wind to ensure rapid dispersal to seaward.

### Marine pollution

The Antarctic is designated as a 'Special Area' under the International Convention for the Prevention of Pollution from Ships (MARPOL 73/78) and the requirements for protection are higher than in most other areas of the sea. Key points to be aware of are that the discharge into the sea of oil, any oily mixture or noxious liquid is prohibited and all sludge, dirty ballast, tank washing waters and other oily residues are required to be retained on board while within the Antarctic Treaty area. At the sub-Antarctic islands, similar rules may also apply within the territorial waters governed by the legislation of the respective countries.

In addition, Annex IV of the Protocol refers to and elaborates on the MARPOL 73/78 requirements, and in July 2007, the International Maritime Organization (IMO) approved Antarctic Ballast Water Guidelines (IMO Resolution MEPC 163 (56)) which apply to all shipping entering Antarctica. The full requirements are detailed. For more information about MARPOL 73/78 and MEPC 163 (56), contact the International Maritime Organization (IMO) (www.imo.org – go to the 'Conventions').

### Emergency situations

During your cruise in Antarctic waters, you are expected to take responsibility and plan accordingly for any eventual accident or change of plan, without having recourse to outside assistance. Of course, a distress call whether via Iridium satellite phone, HF radio on 2128 KHz or 4146 KHz, VHF channel 16 or EPIRB and for whatever reason, will attract an immediate response from all vessels in the vicinity since there are no official search and rescue (SAR) organisations operating south of 60°S. This is all the more reason to ensure that you make every effort to get yourself out of trouble first before initiating an emer-gency call that will inevitably have major repercussions within the international Antarctic community and with your national authority, in addition to those associated with the SAR operation itself.

Aircraft operating between the Antarctic Peninsula and South America (mainly from the Chilean airfield on King George Island) have been used for emergency medical evacuations – adequate insurance cover is vital, as you will be billed!

Remember that there are many areas in the Antarctic that are not fully or accurately surveyed. Marine charts may be incomplete or lacking in precision; uncharted rocks are numerous and present a real danger to navigation; Global Positioning Systems (GPS) coordinates rarely correspond to your position on the chart. Also, navigational errors due to misjudgment of distances are common. Use of radar and depth-sounder with vigilance at all times will reduce the risk of error.

### Use of vehicles and engines

If you intend using a microlite, gyrocopter, plane etc. during your visit, consult the *Guidelines for the Operation of Aircraft Near Concentrations of Birds in Antarctica* (www.comnap.aq/publications/guide lines). In brief, landing and take-off sites should be at least ½ nautical mile (~930 m) from bird colonies and keep at least 2000 ft (~610 m) above any colony. In addition, a *Wildlife Awareness Manual* (www.era.gs/resources/wam) is available for the Antarctic Peninsula / South Shetland Islands / South Orkney Islands region. It provides practical information on wildlife localities to assist aircraft operators avoid sensitive sites as far as practicable, and also shows the locations of protected areas in the region.

If you intend using a Ski-Doo or other snow and ice vehicle, again, keep well clear of any birds and seals. For guidance on use of vessels including aircraft, Zodiacs and kayaks near wildlife concentrations, and when viewing whales at close quarters, refer to the *IAATO Marine Wildlife Watching Guidelines* (see Annex III on p. 118).

**Light pollution**
Seabirds are attracted to bright lights, especially on misty nights when there is a risk of birds colliding with the vessel's superstructure and rigging. When within sight of land and at anchor, and especially in the vicinity of sub-Antarctic islands, keep deck lighting and ice lights to the minimum level required for safe operations and use black-out blinds on portholes and windows.

## Planning site visits and landings

The number of people visiting Antarctica increases each year, and it is not uncommon for several cruise ships, resupply vessels and yachts to be operating in the same area at the same time, notably in the South Shetland Islands and the Gerlache Strait area of the Antarctic Peninsula (Map 2).

Some landing sites here are now being visited three or four times a day by cruise ships. Since some of the best protected yacht anchorages are also near some of the most popular visitor landing sites, you should be aware that other people may be visiting the site at the same time as you. It is possible to find out who will be visiting and when: IAATO member cruise ships have a booking system for their site visits, with landings agreed upon months in advance – see www.iaato.org for each season's shipping schedule, usually posted late October. This information is also included in the annually updated package of information for one-off private yacht expeditions to the Antarctic, available from IAATO. Last-minute changes to the schedule, e.g. due to weather, are not unusual, so if you want to find out who is in the area, listen out on HF 6220 kHz at 19:30 GMT when cruise ships are coordinating the next day's landings.

Keep in mind that IAATO cruise ship landings are highly organised events that usually last three to four hours. They are managed by expedition staff whose job it is to look after up to 100 passengers onshore at any one time, and to ensure that site guidelines and codes of conduct are respected by all. The presence of other visitors ashore at the same time as passengers has the potential to lead to misunderstandings and for this reason, yacht skippers who are regular visitors to the region advise (indeed some insist) that their passengers and crew remain

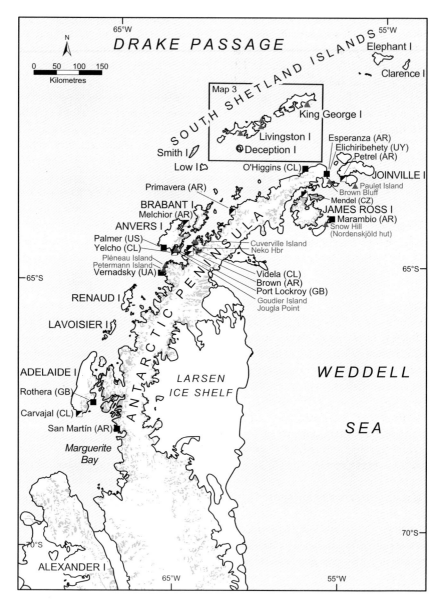

Map 2. The Antarctic Peninsula: permanent stations and sites where Antarctic Treaty
Visitor Site Guidelines apply

on board until the cruise ship has left the anchorage. As standard practice, this is an advisable course of action to take should you find yourself in an anchorage at the same time as a cruise ship.

## Environmental guidelines for landings

Before and after every landing, it is essential that all boots, clothing and equipment be cleaned and where possible dried completely between landings. This is a precautionary measure aimed at preventing the spread of non-native organisms between sites. For more details, see p. 28.

Wherever you go, tread carefully and with awareness, walking slowly when near wildlife. Watch your step in order to avoid inadvertently walking over areas of moss or lichens, or disturbing an aggressive fur seal or a nesting bird that is unaware of your presence. Do not mark areas in any way, for example by erecting rock cairns or leaving mooring chains. Leave an anchorage exactly as you found it, without any trace of your passing.

Many Antarctic and sub-Antarctic birds show little fear of people, and some penguins will even walk right up to you if you sit quietly. Do not however, touch or handle wildlife. Always give birds and seals right-of-way and keep noise to a minimum. Make sure that any photographers or film-makers on board are aware of these guidelines. Activities,

whether scientific, journalistic or purely recreational, should not disrupt the natural behaviour of wildlife: there is no picture, shot or sample that could justify this disturbance.

Wildlife approach distances vary according to species, and region or island – 5 metres is the minimum precautionary distance in the Antarctic but be prepared to increase this distance if any change in behaviour is observed. Some species are extremely sensitive to disturbance during the summer breeding season, and moulting birds in particular should be given a wide berth, since if disturbed they may use up energy reserves that are critical for survival. Some Southern Ocean islands have species-specific distances, so make sure you check with local authorities first.

### Birds

Be aware of the perimeter of seabird colonies and remain at least 5 metres from it, moving slowly and carefully so that the birds are not disturbed. Gentoo penguins, in particular, will easily abandon eggs or chicks if approached within 5 m. Southern giant petrels are particularly sensitive to disturbance, abandoning their nest if approached too closely, and returning some 40-60 minutes later, by which time egg or chick may have succumbed to skua predation or the effects of chilling. Ideally, visits to sites where giant petrels are nesting are best done once the chicks are large enough to look after themselves, which is about from February on. If you inadvertently go ashore where giant petrels are nesting, minimise disturbance by keeping 50 metres away from the birds. If the birds are on a higher level, it may be possible to pass closer than 50 metres without causing birds to leave their nests. Increase these distances if any change in the birds' behaviour is observed.

Kelp gulls and Antarctic terns are equally sensitive, and may abandon their nests at the mere sight of humans. Pay attention to the behaviour of flying birds: 'dive-bombing' by skuas and terns means that you are walking too close to a nest, although you may not have spotted it. Avoid walking through areas where there are kelp gull and skua chicks; once a chick is scared out of its home territory, other gulls or skuas are likely to attack and kill it. Do not feed skuas, gulls and sheathbills, or leave scraps of food where birds could get at them: some birds learn to associate humans with food and in so doing gain an undesirable advantage over other species, many of which they prey on.

## Seals

Crabeater seals commonly haul out on ice floes, Weddell seals on beaches, along with small groups of elephant seals in certain areas, and leopard seals may be seen both on shore and on the ice. Always avoid disturbing these seals, and treat leopard seals with respect: they have been known to attack people in the water and can move very fast on land. Antarctic fur seals are numerous at many sites on the Antarctic Peninsula between January

and March. Keep your distance from them – at least 15 metres is recommended – as they can be aggressive, and a fur seal bite can be deep and is extremely prone to infection. Do not try to pass between them and the water's edge, since this is the direction they will take if disturbed. Fur seals, elephant seals and leopard seals occasionally 'attack' and maul a rubber dinghy; damage can be beyond temporary repair, so unless you are actually in the dinghy, it's a good idea to keep it out of the water.

## Plants

Avoid walking on any vegetation: mosses and lichens are fragile, slow-growing plants that may never recover if damaged or dislodged: a footprint on a moss bank may remain there for longer than your lifetime. Walk carefully around these areas, treading on rocks and snow only, and avoid soft loose gravel and unstable lichen-covered scree slopes. No plants (lichens, moss, grass, pearlwort, algae or fungi) are to be collected.

## Geological features

No rocks, fossils or mineral specimens are to be taken. Where possible, avoid walking on scree slopes, patterned ground and soft soils.

## Preventing the introduction of non-native species

Most Antarctic regions and Southern Ocean islands are uninhabited. Many have retained their pristine natural state, where native wildlife and plants thrive in an environment that remains free of introduced species and undisturbed by humans. One of the greatest threats to these remote regions is the accidental introduction of non-native species of animals (notably rats and mice), plants, invertebrates and micro-organisms. Rodents will reduce and even eliminate seabird populations and small landbirds, invertebrates and plants. Although they are rarely found on yachts, where their presence would be quickly detected, it is absolutely essential to be certain that there are no rats or mice on board before you visit these regions, or when sailing from rodent-infested to rodent-free areas within island groups. Similarly, seeds, invertebrates, spores, viruses and bacteria (for example avian cholera, avian pox, salmonella) in food, food wastes, dirty footwear, clothing or equipment pose a very real threat to native wildlife and plant populations.

By following the simple measures outlined here you can greatly reduce the risk of introductions of alien species. Refer also to the *IAATO Bootwashing and Clothing Decontamination Guidelines* on p. 123. Note that additional or more stringent conditions may apply at some sub-Antarctic islands and the relevant government agency(ies) responsible for these sites should be contacted well before departure to confirm specific requirements.

• All boots, clothing and equipment should be cleaned before and after every landing, and where possible dried completely between landings.

• Where possible, cleaning facilities should be provided on deck – brushes for clothing, boot washing stations equipped with buckets of disinfectant such as strong bleach solution, stiff brushes and running water.

• Discharge of dirty ballast water is prohibited within the Antarctic Treaty area. National regulations apply in the territorial waters of the sub-Antarctic islands.

• Vessel hulls should be cleaned where possible prior to visiting so as to reduce the risk of hull fouling resulting in the introduction of invasive marine species. Similarly, all marine equipment such as inflatables, RIBs, tenders and diving gear should be cleaned prior to departure.

• A current de-ratting certificate is required at most Southern Ocean islands, and vessels should maintain bait stations or traps.

• All vessels berthing alongside a jetty should use rat guards on mooring lines, raise the gangway at night and secure all hatches.

• Food wastes should be disposed of within the Antarctic Treaty area according to the procedures detailed under 'Waste Disposal' on p. 23. National regulations apply in the territorial waters of the sub-Antarctic islands.

• No foodstuffs should be left on deck. Food scraps should not be fed to birds or mammals.

• Special care must be taken with waste animal products: all residues of imported animals and particularly of poultry products (e.g. chicken bones, eggs) must be removed from the Antarctic Treaty area unless sterilised (see p. 23). Note that no poultry products are allowed at the sub-Antarctic islands of Gough, Marion, Prince Edward, Heard, McDonald, Macquarie, Campbell, Antipodes, Bounty, Snares and Auckland.

- Precautions should be taken when packing cargo in areas where rodents and invertebrates may be present.
- Regular inspections for the presence of rodents and invertebrates should be made during cargo handling.
- Food destined for shore-based field parties should be packed in rodent- and ideally invertebrate-proof containers.

## Facilities and structures

### Rock cairns and depots

Rock cairns erected by explorers and scientists over the past century for use as depot markers, trigonometrical stations for mapping, and even as a letterbox, are now of historical interest. Many have been designated as Historic Sites and Monuments under the Antarctic Treaty, and as such must not be damaged, removed or destroyed. Those that have not been designated should also be left undisturbed, and should you find anything that has not previously been discovered then you should notify the appropriate authorities in your home country. A rock cairn or marker pole may also indicate a field depot of food boxes and fuel cached by personnel for emergency use during summer and winter excursions. This material is for emergency

use only and should not be disturbed in any way. If you notice anything amiss with the depot it can be of help to report it to the nearest station responsible.

### Historic buildings and unoccupied stations

A number of early stations and field huts that are no longer operational have been designated as Historic Sites and Monuments. Some of these have also been designated with specially protected status, with access allowed by prior permit only: should you wish to visit one of these sites you should seek a permit in advance. Even some of those that do not have specially protected status are kept locked, although the key is usually easily obtainable from a nearby operational station. Historic sites that require permits for entry are listed as Antarctic Specially Protected Areas (see below).

Other buildings that are not designated and yet may appear disused may in fact be occupied intermittently by expedition parties for various lengths of time. The few completely abandoned stations and huts are easily recognised by their extreme state of disrepair and in recent years a number of them have been removed.

If you should enter one of these buildings – whether it is a designated Historic Site or Monument or not – make sure that one member of your party is responsible for shutting all doors and windows after the last person has left. A door left open means a building full of snow at the end of the next winter, a lot of work for the next occupant and leads to a rapid deterioration of the structure. Avoid smoking in or near these buildings: the wood is generally very dry and can easily catch fire. Again, if you notice anything amiss at a hut – a broken window, leaking roof etc. – it can be of help to report it to the nearest station. Check out the location of Historic Sites and Monuments in Annex VI (p. 130) and at the Antarctic Protected Areas Information Archive (http://cep.ats.aq/cep/apa/index.html).

## Occupied stations

If you intend visiting a station, it is strongly advised that you contact the station's radio operator or station leader by VHF radio on channels 12 or 16 prior to arrival, requesting permission to visit the station, and stating your estimated time of arrival and number of people aboard.

Some stations, for example Palmer Station (US), limit the number of cruise ship visits and the season's visit schedule is agreed well in advance. While this does not presently apply to yachts, be aware that all visits to stations have the potential to place additional demands on limited time and resources of scientific programmes, and with increasing numbers this can have a cumulative effect.

It is standard IAATO practice for tour operators to notify station leaders of an intended visit 72 hours in advance. Similar advance notice by yachts can also be helpful to stations so they can anticipate and, if necessary, coordinate visits. On

landing at some stations you may be greeted by the station leader. Other stations may leave it up to you to find your way to the person in charge, but in all instances it is essential first to make contact with the station leader, either by radio and / or upon landing. Remember that you are entering a small community of people for whom the station is home, and whose 'backyard' also includes the anchorage you are using. It is also essential to check with the station leader about research sites in the immediate vicinity of the station. Find out if there are sites that should be avoided and always ask permission before wandering around. If you do come across any instruments or study sites, do not disturb them. These sites may be in addition to the Antarctic Specially Protected Areas and Antarctic Specially Managed Areas that are described below.

Bear in mind that station personnel are employed full-time maintaining equipment and running the station; some, particularly where scientific programs are carried out, will be working shifts around the clock. For these reasons, it is preferable to time your visits ashore towards the end of the day, unless otherwise advised by the station leader. Also, your visit could coincide with the arrival of a cruise ship, a supply vessel or a period of intensive work, all of which may take precedence over your visit. It is suggested that you limit your stay at the station's anchorage and immediate environs to 24 hours, weather permitting. There are plenty of other anchorages in which you can wait, rest or repair, whatever is the case. Your presence at a station, however discrete, will always be, at best, a welcome social distraction but should not test the limits of hospitality. Do not expect hospitality to include an invitation to dine or to take showers, fuel, water, food or other supplies. Remember that there will be other yachts calling in too, so don't overstay your welcome. Reciprocation of hospitality offered by the station is always appreciated.

**Scientific equipment and instrumentation**

Scientific projects frequently install equipment or instrumentation for experiments or monitoring purposes and these should not be disturbed. Some of these experiments may be carried out over long periods of time, and equipment can deteriorate or become damaged in the harsh conditions. Even so, installations should not be disturbed even if you think that it looks abandoned, unless there is an obvious threat to wildlife, plants or other important resources; instead, notify the appropriate national authority of what you have observed as it is their responsibility to ensure the problem is addressed.

## Site management

While the Antarctic Treaty area as a whole has special conservation status, additional protection is given to particularly special or vulnerable sites. There are three main categories of protection or site management within the Antarctic Treaty

area: Antarctic Specially Protected Areas (ASPAs), Antarctic Specially Managed Areas (ASMAs) and Historic Sites and Monuments (HSMs). These categories replace the former categories of Specially Protected Area (SPA), Site of Special Scientific Interest (SSSI) and Multiple-use Planning Area, although you may find the old categories are frequently referred to on maps and in the literature. In addition, Antarctic Treaty Visitor Site Guidelines have been prepared for a number of frequently visited sites. These Site Guidelines are designed to inform people about local sensitivities and features and to avoid disturbance to the site and its wildlife. A complete list of all sites with their respective forms of designation (as at October 2007) is included in Annex V on p. 126.

Note that entry into an ASPA is prohibited except by permit, and this special permit is additional to any that is needed to visit Antarctica in general. Nationals of each country signatory to the Antarctic Treaty can apply to their respective Antarctic national committee or institute for a permit. Entry into an ASMA does not require a special permit but activities there are guided by a Code of Conduct set out in each area's Management Plan.

ASPAs are designated "to protect outstanding environmental, scientific, historic, aesthetic or wilderness values, any combination of those values, or ongoing or planned scientific research". ASMAs may include "areas where activities pose

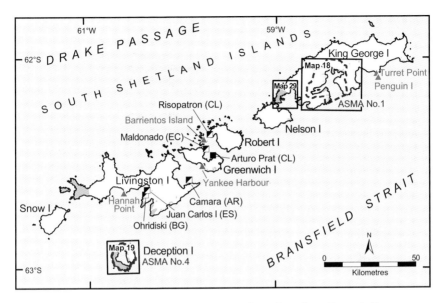

Map 3. The South Shetland Islands: permanent stations, sites where Antarctic Treaty
Visitor Site Guidelines apply, and Antarctic Specially Managed Areas

risks of mutual interference or cumulative environmental impacts, as well as sites or monuments of recognised historical value". Information on ASPAs and ASMAs is included in the sections below.

At the time of writing, 78 Historic Sites and Monuments (HSMs) were recognised under the Antarctic Treaty (see Annex VI on p.130 for a complete list). Most do not require any special visiting arrangements. Be aware, however, that some of the most sensitive and popular historic sites are also ASPAs, and that access to these is only allowed by permit in accordance with conditions set out in their management plans. For more information about ASPAs, ASMAs and HSMs, refer also to the online Antarctic

Protected Areas Information Archive (http:// cep.ats.aq/cep/apa/index.html).

Note that it is the responsibility of the skipper and / or organiser to ensure that passengers and crew are aware of the locations of these ASPAs, ASMAs and HSMs, and of the restrictions that apply to these areas. You should also be aware that in addition to these and the Antarctic Treaty Visitor Site Guidelines, informal local guidelines may apply at areas close to stations. As part of your cruise preparation, it is advisable to check relevant websites for the latest information, especially on www.ats.aq (under 'Topics' > 'Other'), and when on site to ask station leaders about the latest procedures to follow.

## Antarctic Treaty Visitor Site Guidelines

Visits to some of the most popular landing sites on the Antarctic Peninsula (Map 2), and especially in the South Shetland Islands (Map 3), are now subject to site-specific guidelines. No special permit is required to visit these areas, but the Site Guidelines must be followed. Although primarily aimed at vessels carrying more than 12 passengers, the Site Guidelines are also relevant to smaller groups. They provide tour operators, expedition leaders and guides with site-specific information and practical guidance on how visits should be conducted at the most popular destinations, taking into account their particular environmental values and sensitivities.

At the time of writing, Site Guidelines have been adopted for 14 sites by the Treaty Parties, with the expectation that additional sites will be included in the future. For most of these sites it is recommended that people avoid going ashore between 22:00hrs and 04:00hrs local time (GMT-3 hours) to provide a resting period for wildlife. Visits to Port Lockroy should be between 07:00 and 18:00 (local time), and to the historic hut at Snow Hill between 08:00 and 19:00 hrs (local time).

The full text of the Site Guidelines for each site agreed to date is provided below, together with selected maps. However, it is essential that you obtain up-to-date information and guidelines for more recently agreed sites. For each site, a one-page summary of key guidelines with colour maps and photographs can be downloaded from the Antarctic Treaty website (www.ats.aq under 'Topics' > 'Other'). For additional descriptions of some of these sites see also *The Oceanites Site Guide to the Antarctic Peninsula* (Naveen 2005) and the Oceanites website www.oceanites.org.

## Paulet Island

Topography

This circular island is 1.6 km in diameter. It has a distinct volcanic cone that rises to a height of 350 metres. A flat terrace forms an apron around the north and northeast side of the island. At high tide, this terrace is largely submerged, severely restricting visitor space.

Fauna

*Confirmed breeders:* Adélie penguin (*Pygoscelis adeliae*), blue-eyed shag (*Phalacrocorax atriceps*), kelp gull (*Larus dominicanus*) and snowy sheathbill (*Chionis alba*).
*Likely breeders:* Snow petrel (*Pagodroma nivea*) and Wilson's storm-petrel (*Oceanites oceanicus*).
*Regularly haul out:* Weddell seals (*Leptonychotes weddellii*) and Antarctic fur seals (*Arctocephalus gazella*) (the latter potentially in large numbers from February onwards). Leopard seals (*Hydrurga leptonyx*) often hunt offshore.

Other

Stone hut, grave and cairn (Historic Site and Monument No.41).

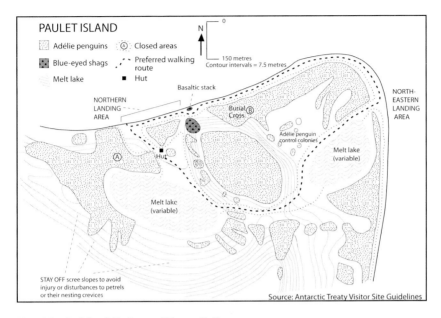

**Map 4. Paulet Island, Erebus and Terror Gulf**

Visitor impact

*Known impacts:* None.

*Potential impacts:* Disturbance of wildlife, particularly Adélie penguins, and damage to the historic site.

Landing requirements

*Ships (A ship is defined as a vessel which carries more than 12 passengers.)*

• Ships carrying 200 or fewer passengers

• One ship at a time.

• Maximum 2 ships per day (midnight to midnight).

*Visitors*

• No more than 100 visitors at any time. However, at high tide, no more than 50 visitors at any time in the area around the northern coast landing site.

• Maximum visitor numbers are exclusive of expedition guides and leaders, maintaining a minimum ratio of 1 guide to 20 visitors.

• No visitors ashore between 22:00hrs and 04:00hrs (local time). This is in order to establish a rest period for wildlife.

Visitor area

*Landing Area*

• Cobble landing beaches on either the northern or northeastern coast. Landing may be impossible late in the season, if Antarctic fur seals are present in large numbers.

35

*Closed areas*
- Closed Area A: Loose steep scree slopes which are densely packed with breeding Adélie penguins. Snow petrels and Wilson's storm petrels strongly suspected of breeding in the scree.
- Closed Area B: Densely packed area to the northeast of the island, with breeding Adélie penguins and blue-eyed shags, including Adélie penguin control colonies.

*Guided walking areas*
Because of restricted visitor space, all walks at this site should be carefully controlled in guided groups of no more than 15-20 visitors. Groups should be well-spaced and follow the designated paths along the northern coast, or towards the historic hut and the volcanic, ovoid lake.

*Free roaming areas*
None.

## Brown Bluff

Topography
1.5 km long cobble and ash beach rising increasingly steeply towards towering red-brown tuff cliffs which are embedded with volcanic bombs. The cliffs are heavily eroded, resulting in loose scree and rock falls on higher slopes and large, wind eroded boulders on the beach. At high water the beach area can be restricted. Permanent ice and tidewater glaciers surround the site to the north and south occasionally filling the beach with brash ice.

Fauna
*Confirmed breeders:* Gentoo penguin (*Pygoscelis papua*), Adélie penguin (*Pygoscelis adeliae*), pintado petrel (*Daption capense*), snow petrel (*Pagodroma nivea*), skuas (*Catharacta* spp.) and kelp gull (*Larus dominicanus*). *Suspected breeders:* Southern giant petrel (*Macronectes giganteus*), southern fulmar (*Fulmarus glacialoides*) and Wilson's storm-petrel (*Oceanites oceanicus*). *Regularly haul out:* Weddell seals (*Leptonychotes weddellii*). Leopard seals (*Hydrurga leptonyx*) often hunt offshore.

Flora
*Xanthoria* spp. and *Caloplaca* spp. observed on exposed boulders from shoreline to an elevation of 606 feet. Some moss species exposed at higher elevations near glacial drainage.

Other
Hazardous rocks and reefs lie immediately off shore.

Visitor impact
*Known impacts:* None
*Potential impacts:* Disturbance of wildlife, especially kelp gulls.

Landing requirements
*Ships (A ship is defined as a vessel which carries more than 12 passengers.):*
- Ships carrying 500 or fewer passengers.

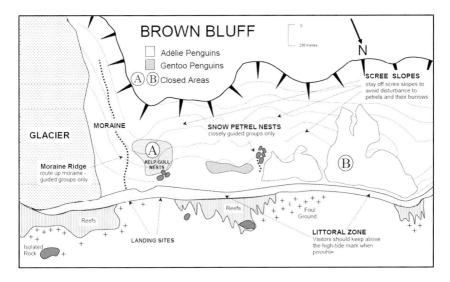

Map 5. Brown Bluff, Antarctic Sound

- One ship at a time.
- Maximum 3 ships per day (midnight to midnight), of which no more than 1 may be a vessel carrying more than 200 passengers.

*Visitors*
- No more than 100 visitors ashore at any time, exclusive of expedition guides and leaders.
- 1 guide per 20 visitors.
- No visitors ashore between 22:00hrs and 04:00hrs (local time). This is in order to establish a resting period for the wildlife.

Visitor area
*Landing area:*
- Primary: The southern end of the beach to the east of the three large boulders

at the northern end of the snow slope – protected by two reefs.

*Closed areas*
- Closed Area A: Kelp gull colony in the boulder area behind the landing beach, extending from the three large boulders up the small gully running SSE behind the moraine ridge.
- Closed Area B: Area of densely packed breeding Adélie penguins at north end of beach.

*Guided walking areas*
Elevated areas behind the landing beach. Visits to the snow petrel nests on the slopes behind the penguin rookeries should be done in closely guided groups with a ratio of 1 guide to 12 passengers – where the guide knows the location

37

of the nests in advance. Care should be taken not to disturb loose rocks. Groups visiting the moraine ridge along the edge of the snow slope to the east of the landing beach should be closely guided to avoid disturbance to skua nests up on the high ground.

*Free roaming areas*
Visitors may roam freely along the main flat beach area between landing site to the south and the closed areas.
Note: the littoral zone up to the high tide mark is often used as an access route by Adelie penguins. Visitors should be kept above the high water mark.

Visitor Code of Conduct
*Behaviour ashore*
• Walk slowly and carefully.
• Maintain a precautionary distance of 5 metres from wildlife and give animals the right-of-way. Increase this distance if any change in behaviour is observed.
• Take care not to disturb kelp gull nesting sites.
• Be careful around Antarctic fur seals, they may be aggressive.
• Take care not to displace penguins along the shoreline. Keep visitors above the high tide mark and at high water be aware it may be necessary to have visitors walk in small groups escorted by staff.

*Cautionary notes*
• Strong and katabatic winds are a feature of this area, and pack and brash

ice are frequently blown onto the beach area.
• Rock falls occur from the cliffs and steeper scree slopes.
• The primary landing beach may be crowded with wildlife. Landing beach is prone to swells from N and NE.

## Snow Hill, Nordenskjöld Hut
Topography
The hut is found on the northeast coast of Snow Hill Island. The relief is characterised by three distinct units: the topography gradually rises from the coastline to the 5-10 m contour in terraced sedimentary levels. On one of these is found the Nordenskjöld hut. From there up to the 170 m contour, the relief consists of steep slopes (15-40°), which are highly dissected by deep fluvial valleys. This area has abundant fossils of marine origin and is traversed by basalt dikes that run NE-SW. Due to their greater resistance to erosion, these constitute important topographic features. The most important feature is Haslum Crag, a small volcanic neck. At the 170 m contour, the topography descends gradually to the Weddell Sea.

Fauna
*Confirmed breeders:* 3-5 nests of kelp gull (*Larus dominicanus*) and Antarctic tern (Sterna vittata) 500 metres northeast of the hut on the northwest facing slope.

Flora
Virtually absent.

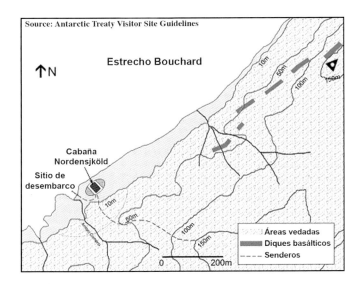

Source: Antarctic Treaty Visitor Site Guidelines

Map 6. Nordenskjöld Hut, Snow Hill Island

Other

Wooden hut on Snow Hill Island built in February 1902 by the main party of the Swedish South Polar Expedition led by Otto Nordenskjöld. It was designated as Historic Site and Monument number 38 in the framework of the Antarctic Treaty. The hut contains original objects from the expedition and functions as a living museum, which is managed by Argentina and Sweden.

Visitor impact

Known impacts: Some acts of vandalism in the hut's interior have been recorded. Potential impacts: Worsening of erosive processes – naturally rapid in the area of the location of the hut – due to trampling. Fire. Small fuel leaks.

Landing requirements

Ships (A ship is defined as a vessel which carries more than 12 passengers.)
• Ships carrying 500 or fewer passengers aboard
• One ship at a time.
• Ships should contact the hut with 24 hours of anticipation to confirm the visit.

Visitors
• No more than 100 visitors ashore at any time.
• Maximum visitor numbers are exclusive of expedition guides and leaders.
• 1 guide for every 20 visitors.
• Visits to the hut may only be made with the prior agreement of the head of the hut.
• Visits to the interior of the hut should be

39

conducted in groups of no more than 5 persons at a time.
• No visitors to the hut between 19:00 and 08:00 hrs (local time).

Visitor area
*Landing area*
• On the beach facing the hut, northeast of the Comerci channel (see map).

*Closed areas*
• Closed area A: The northeast and southwestern ends of the small terrace on which the hut is located, to avoid the acceleration of erosive processes. These areas are clearly marked with stakes and rope.
• Closed area B: The entire area with steep slopes, with the exception of the ascending path. This area has important paleontological deposits.

*Guided walking areas*
Visitors should use the path that is shown in the map to go to the hut and return to the landing area. To climb the terrace on which the hut is found, they should use the stairs. More than 10 persons at a time are not permitted on the terrace on which the hut is located. Ascent of the slope that is behind the hut will be carried out using the path (see map) marked by a row of flags. The final section has a fixed rope to assist visitors in completing the ascent. Given that the slope is steep, groups that use the path cannot exceed 10 people at a time and should be assisted by a guide .

*Free roaming areas*
Visitors can move freely under supervision along the glaciofluvial plain around the landing site and extending southwest of the Comerci channel (see map). The free roaming area ends at the slope ridge.

Visitor Code of Conduct
*Behaviour ashore*
• Be careful around the hut and on the small terrace on which it sits.
• Do not step on, move or damage the structures built to prop up the foundations of the hut. Before entering the hut, visitors should clean their boots. Removing snow and humidity from clothes and backpacks is recommended. Do not touch any object that is on display or the personal items of people living in the hut or in associated camps.
• Smoking is strictly prohibited.
• Collection of fossils or any other type of material from the ground is prohibited.

*Cautionary notes*
• Be extremely cautious when climbing the slope southeast of the hut.

## Turret Point on King George Island
Topography
Turret Point is marked by conspicuous rock stacks that form the eastern limit of King George Bay west of Three Sisters Point. There is a cobble beach on the southern coast and melt pools inland. The beach gently slopes to an extensive, heavily crevassed glacier.

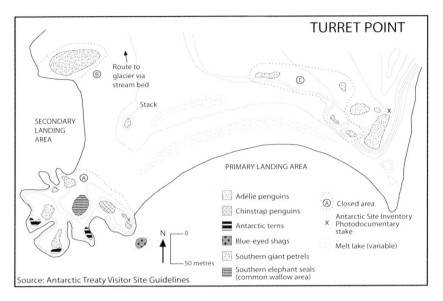

**Map 7. Turret Point, King George Island**

Fauna
*Confirmed breeders:* Adélie penguin
(*Pygoscelis adeliae*), chinstrap penguin
(*Pygoscelis antarctica*), southern giant
petrel (*Macronectes giganteus*), kelp gull
(*Larus dominicanus*), blue-eyed shag
(*Phalacrocorax atriceps*), and Antarctic
tern (*Sterna vittata*).
*Suspected breeders:* Skuas (*Catharacta*
spp.) and snowy sheathbill (*Chionis alba*).
*Regularly wallow and haul out:* southern
elephant seal (*Mirounga leonina*), Weddell
seals (*Leptonychotes weddellii*) and
Antarctic fur seals (*Arctocephalus gazella*).

Flora
Swards of moss species, the lichens
*Xanthoria* spp., *Caloplaca* spp. and other
crustose lichens.

Visitor impact
*Known impacts:* None.
*Potential impacts:* Trampling of vegetation
en route to the glacier and disturbance
of wildlife, particularly southern giant
petrels.

Landing requirements
*Ships (A ship is defined as a vessel which
carries more than 12 passengers.)*
• Ships carrying 200 or fewer passengers
• One ship at a time.
• Maximum 2 ships per day (midnight to
  midnight).

*Visitors*
• No more than 100 visitors ashore at
  once, exclusive of expedition guides
  and leaders.

41

- 1 guide per 20 visitors.
- No visitors ashore between 22:00hrs and 04:00hrs (local time). This is in order to establish a rest period for wildlife.

### Visitor area
*Landing area*
- Primary: along an exposed broad cobble beach to the south, which may be packed with ice.
- Secondary: to the west. If this is used, be sure to stay clear of nesting sites for southern giant petrel at both ends of the beach (Closed Areas A and B).

*Closed areas*
- Closed Area A: Biodiverse fragile area including nesting southern giant petrels, kelp gulls, chinstrap penguins, blue-eyed shags and elephant seals wallows.
- Closed Area B: Nesting southern giant petrels.
- Closed Area C: Elevated area above the beach with nesting southern giant petrels.

*Guided walking areas*
Visitors to the glacier should be guided in small groups following the streambed to avoid trampling of vegetation.

*Free roaming areas*
Visitors may roam freely, but under supervision, between the landing beaches, avoiding the closed areas.

### Visitor Code of Conduct
*Behaviour ashore*
- Walk slowly and carefully.
- Maintain a precautionary distance of 5 metres from wildlife and give animals the right-of-way. Increase this distance if any change in behaviour is observed.
- When on the same level as, or higher than, nesting southern giant petrels maintain a precautionary distance of at least 50 metres. Increase this distance if any change in the birds' behaviour is observed.
- Be careful near Antarctic fur seals, they may be aggressive.
- Do not walk on any vegetation.

Cautionary notes
- While weather conditions can change rapidly anywhere in the Antarctic, this location is particularly prone to such changes.

## Penguin Island
Topography
This oval island is 1.6km long. The site's prominent geological feature is the 170m high cone of Deacon Peak, the northern face of which slopes gently down to the landing beach. Most of the island is surrounded by low cliffs, and there is a crater lake in the northeast.

Fauna
*Confirmed breeders:* Chinstrap penguin (*Pygoscelis antarctica*), Adélie penguin (*Pygoscelis adeliae*), southern giant petrel (*Macronectes giganteus*), Antarctic

tern (*Sterna vittata*), kelp gull (*Larus dominicanus*), and skuas (*Catharacta* spp.). *Likely breeders:* Snowy sheathbill (*Chionis alba*) and Wilson's storm petrel (*Oceanites oceanicus*). *Regular roosting:* Blue-eyed shags (*Phalacrocorax atriceps*). *Regularly haul out:* Southern elephant seals (*Mirounga leonina*) and Weddell seals (*Leptonychotes weddellii*).

Flora
*Deschampsia antarctica, Colobanthus quitensis, Xanthoria elegans,* moss

species, *Caloplaca* and other crustose lichen species, and large swards of the fruticose lichen *Usnea antarctica.*

Visitor impact
*Known impacts:* Erosion of footpaths en route to Deacon Peak.
*Potential impacts:* Trampling of vegetation, and disturbance of wildlife, particularly southern giant petrels.

Landing requirements
*Ships (A ship is defined as a vessel which carries more than 12 passengers.)*

**Map 8. Penguin Island**

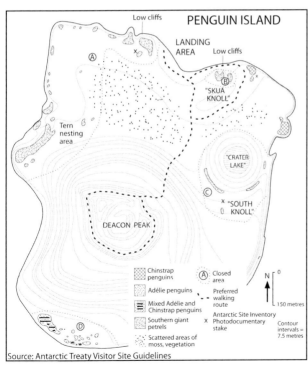

Source: Antarctic Treaty Visitor Site Guidelines

43

- Ships carrying 200 or fewer passengers.
- One ship at a time.
- Maximum 2 ships per day (midnight to midnight).

*Visitors*
- No more than 100 visitors ashore at any time, exclusive of expedition guides and leaders.
- 1 guide per 20 visitors.
- No visitors ashore between 22:00hrs and 04:00hrs (local time). This is in order to establish a rest period for wildlife.

Visitor area
*Landing area*
- The broad cobble beach along the northern coast. Be sure to land well clear of the low cliffs to the west of the landing beach because of the nesting southern giant petrels (Closed Area A).

*Closed areas*
- Closed Area A: Northwestern area of the island and low cliffs along the northern coastline where southern giant petrels nest.
- Closed Area B: Vicinity of low cliff at the northeastern end of the island, where southern giant petrels nest.
- Closed Area C: Rim of "crater lake" and knolls to the south, which have dense vegetation and where southern giant petrels nest.
- Closed Area D: Monitoring control sites for penguins at the southern end of the island.

*Guided walking areas*
Those visiting the chinstrap colonies at the northern end of the island should be under close supervision along the cobble shoreline. Particular caution should be exercised in guiding visitors quietly and slowly along the beach to the north of Closed Area B, to avoid disturbing the nesting southern giant petrels on the ledges above. Visitors to Deacon Peak should be directed toward the designated path to the west of Closed Area B. From the chinstrap colony it is also possible to follow the route south of "Skua Knoll". However, this route should only be taken in small guided groups to avoid trampling the vegetation.

*Free roaming areas*
None.

Visitor Code of Conduct
*Behaviour ashore*
- Walk slowly and carefully.
- Maintain a precautionary distance of 5 metres from wildlife and give animals the right-of-way.
- Increase this distance if any change in behaviour is observed.
- When on the same level as, or higher than, nesting southern giant petrels, maintain a precautionary distance of at least 50 metres. Increase this distance if any change in the birds' behaviour is observed.
- Be careful near Antarctic fur seals, they may be aggressive.
- Do not walk on any vegetation.

*Cautionary notes*
• While weather conditions can change rapidly anywhere in the Antarctic, this location is particularly prone to such changes.

## Barrientos Island in the Aitcho Islands

Topography
This 1.5km island's north coast is dominated by steep cliffs, reaching a height of approximately 70 metres, with a gentle slope down to the south coast. The eastern and western ends of the island are black sand and cobbled beaches. Columnar basalt outcrops are a notable feature of the western end.

Fauna
*Confirmed breeders:* Gentoo penguin (*Pygoscelis papua*), chinstrap penguin (*Pygoscelis antarctica*), southern giant petrel (*Macronectes giganteus*), kelp gull (*Larus dominicanus*), and skuas (*Catharacta* spp.).
*Suspected breeders:* Blue-eyed shag (*Phalacrocorax atriceps*) and Wilson's storm-petrel (*Oceanites oceanicus*).
*Regularly haul out:* Weddell seals (*Leptonychotes weddellii*), southern elephant seals (*Mirounga leonina*), and

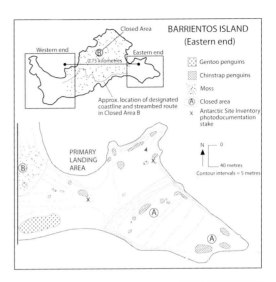

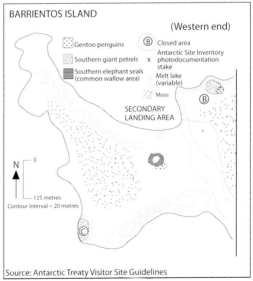

Source: Antarctic Treaty Visitor Site Guidelines

**Map 9. Barrientos Island, Aitcho Islands**

45

from late December Antarctic fur seals (*Arctocephalus gazella*).

Flora
The entire centre of the island is covered by a very extensive moss carpet. Lichens *Xanthoria* spp., *Caloplaca* spp. and other crustose lichen species are present. The green alga *Prasiola crispa* is widespread.

Visitor impact
*Known impacts:* The erosion of multiple footpaths through vegetation between the eastern and western ends of the island.
*Potential impacts:* Further damage to the vegetation and disturbance of wildlife, particularly southern giant petrels.

Landing requirements
*Ships (A ship is defined as a vessel which carries more than 12 passengers.)*
• Ships carrying 200 or fewer passengers.
• One ship at a time.
• Maximum 2 ships per day (midnight to midnight).

*Visitors*
• No more than 100 visitors ashore at any time, exclusive of expedition guides and leaders.
• 1 guide per 20 visitors.
• No visitors ashore between 22:00hrs and 04:00hrs (local time). This is in order to establish a resting period for the wildlife.

Visitor area
*Landing area*
• Primary: eastern end of the island; landing either on the sand beach to the north, or on the cobbled southern beach.
• Secondary: northern shore of the western end of the island, with easiest access at high water.

*Closed areas*
• Closed Area A: Monitoring sites for chinstrap penguins above and southeast of the eastern landing area.
• Closed Area B: Central part of the island covered by a very extensive moss carpet (with the exception of the designated walking route) and the northern cliffs where southern giant petrels nest.
• Closed Area C: Knoll on the southwestern tip of the island where southern giant petrels nest.

*Guided walking areas*
Only walk through Closed Area B if you can clearly recognise the designated route, which runs over the rocks along the shoreline at the eastern end, and along a narrow gravel stream bed through the vegetation. This route should only be used by closely guided groups of no more than 10 visitors. Only one group should follow the stream bed at a time, taking extreme care not to trample the edges of the vegetation.

*Free roaming areas*
Visitors can roam freely, but under

supervision, anywhere except the closed or guided walking areas.

*Behaviour ashore*
• Walk slowly and carefully.
• Maintain a precautionary distance of 5 metres from wildlife and give animals the right-of-way. Increase this distance if any change in behaviour is observed.
• When on the same level as, or higher than, nesting southern giant petrels maintain a precautionary distance of at least 50 metres. Increase this distance if any change in the birds' behaviour is observed.
• Be careful near Antarctic fur seals, they may be aggressive. Do not walk on any vegetation.

*Cautionary notes*
• Stay clear of cliffs and vertical walls and stacks as these are prone to rock falls and slides.

## Yankee Harbour at Greenwich Island

Topography
A small glacial-edged harbour, enclosed by a curved gravel spit. A large terraced beach area includes a melt-pool to the east. Beyond the beach, steep scree slopes rise to a rugged knife-edge summit.

**Map 10. Yankee Harbour, Greenwich Island**

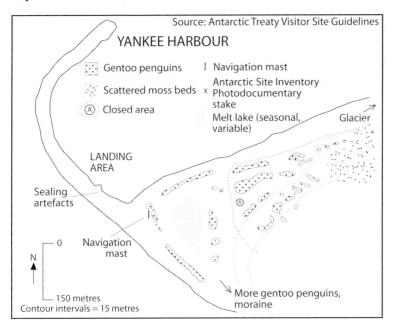

47

Fauna
*Confirmed breeders:* Gentoo penguin
(*Pygoscelis papua*) and skuas (*Catharacta*
spp.).
*Suspected breeders:* Snowy sheathbill
(*Chionis alba*) and Wilson's storm-petrel
(*Oceanites oceanicus*).
*Regularly haul out:* Southern elephant
seals (*Mirounga leonina*), Weddell seals
(*Leptonychotes weddellii*), and Antarctic
fur seals (*Arctocephalus gazella*).

Flora
*Deschampsia antarctica, Colobanthus
quitensis*, swards of moss species,
*Xanthoria* spp. and other crustose lichens,
and the green alga *Prasiola crispa*.

Other
Artefacts from early sealing activities
may be found along the inner shoreline.

Visitor impact
*Known impacts:* None.
*Potential impacts:* Disturbance of wildlife,
damage to the sealing remains and
trampling vegetation.

Landing requirements
*Ships (A ship is defined as a vessel which
carries more than 12 passengers.)*
• Ships carrying 500 or fewer passengers.
• One ship at a time.
• No more than 3 ships carrying more
  than 200 passengers per day (midnight
  to midnight).

*Visitors*
• No more than 100 visitors ashore at

once, exclusive of expedition guides
and leaders.
• 1 guide per 20 visitors.
• No visitors ashore between 22:00hrs
  and 04:00hrs (local time), except for
  those engaged in organised overnight
  stays. This is in order to establish a
  resting period for the wildlife.

Visitor area
*Landing area*
• Along the gravel spit, preferably on the
  inside.

*Closed areas*
• Raised terraces above the melt pool
  with nesting gentoo penguins and the
  scree slopes above.

*Guided walking areas*
None.

*Free roaming areas*
Visitors may roam freely under
supervision anywhere on the site,
except for the closed area. Longer
walks are possible along the curved
spit, towards the glacial moraine on the
southeastern side, and towards
the glacier in the northeast.

Visitor Code of Conduct
*Behaviour ashore*
• Walk slowly and carefully.
• Maintain a precautionary distance
  of 5 metres from wildlife and give
  animals the right-of-way. Increase this
  distance if any change in behaviour
  is observed.

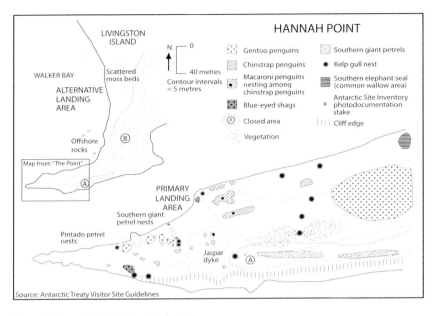

Map 11. Hannah Point, Livingston Island

- Be careful near Antarctic fur seals, they may be aggressive.
- Do not walk on any vegetation.

*Cautionary notes*
- Be careful around the sealing remains to avoid damage and do not move any artefacts.
- Be careful of the wires around the navigational mast. Be aware that glacier calving may produce dangerous waves.

## Hannah Point on Livingston Island
Topography
Hannah Point (the Point) is a narrow peninsula undulating upward to knife-edged ridges and vertical cliff edges 30-50 metres above sea level. There is loose scree on higher slopes and ridges, evidence of rock falls, and a Jaspar mineral vein. Ash-covered slopes link the Point to the flat open beach area of Walker Bay.

Fauna
*Confirmed breeders:* Chinstrap (*Pygoscelis antarctica*), gentoo (*Pygoscelis papua*), and macaroni penguin (*Eudyptes chrysolophus*), blue-eyed shag (*Phalacrocorax atriceps*), snowy sheathbill (*Chionis alba*), kelp gull (*Larus dominicanus*), Antarctic tern (*Sterna vittata*), Wilson's storm-petrel (*Oceanites oceanicus*), Black-bellied storm-petrels (*Fregetta tropica*), pintado petrel (*Daption capense*), skuas (*Catharacta* spp.), and

49

southern giant petrel (*Macronectes giganteus*).
*Regularly haul out:* Southern elephant seal (*Mirounga leonina*), Weddell seals (*Leptonychotes weddellii*) and Antarctic fur seals (*Arctocephalus gazella*).

Flora
Vegetation covers the upper slopes of the Point. *Deschampsia antarctica*, *Colobanthus quitensis*, *Xanthoria* spp. and other crustose lichens are present. The green alga *Prasiola crispa* is widespread. Large moss patches cover Walker Bay.

Other
Some fossil and rock specimens may be observed towards the eastern end of the flat open beach area of Walker Bay.

Visitor impact
*Known impacts:* The erosion of a footpath between the Point and Walker Bay.
*Potential impacts:* Erosion and disturbance of vegetation and wildlife, especially as visitor space is limited on the Point.

Landing requirements
*Ships (A ship is defined as a vessel which carries more than 12 passengers.)*
• Ships carrying 200 or fewer passengers.
• One ship at a time.
• The Point: Given the limited space at this site, visits are strongly discouraged from the start of the breeding season (October) until after early penguin incubation phase (mid-January). After then, maximum 1 ship per day (midnight to midnight).

• Visits to last no longer than 6 hours.
• Walker Bay: a maximum of 2 ships per day (midnight to midnight).

*Visitors*
• No more than 100 visitors at any time, exclusive of expedition guides and leaders, with not more than 50 on the Point.
• 1 guide per 20 visitors.
• No visitors on the Point between 22:00hrs and 04:00hrs (local time).

Visitor area
*Landing area*
• Primary: The small cobble beach on the northern coast of Hannah Point.
• Secondary: If conditions permit, an alternative landing area is the flat open area of Walker Bay, to the north of the Point.

*Closed areas*
• Closed Area A: Cliff area with nesting southern giant petrels.
• Closed Area B: Rocky outcrops with nesting southern giant petrels, including a 50 metre buffer zone.

*Guided walking areas*
Because of restricted visitor space, all walks around the Point should be strictly controlled in guided groups of no more than 15-20 visitors, which are well spaced and which follow the same path. Visitors walking between the Point and Walker Bay should proceed in single file in small groups, avoiding wildlife and other sensitive features.

*Free roaming areas*
Visitors may roam freely, but under supervision, on the beach in Walker Bay, avoiding Closed Area B.

Visitor Code of Conduct
*Behaviour ashore*
• Walk slowly and carefully.
• Maintain a precautionary distance of 5 metres from wildlife and give animals the right-of-way. Increase this distance if any change in behaviour is observed.
• When on the same level as, or higher than, nesting southern giant petrels maintain a precautionary distance of at least 50 metres. Increase this distance if any change in the birds' behaviour is observed.
• Be careful near Antarctic fur seals, they may be aggressive. Do not walk on any vegetation.

*Cautionary notes*
• The primary landing beach may be crowded with wildlife – under such circumstances it would be mot possible to make a landing and maintain the required precautionary distances.
• Both landing beaches are prone to swells.
• Be careful near the jasper dyke. It is brittle and may crumble.
• Exercise particular caution not to disturb animals near cliff edges. If they are disturbed, they may retreat and fall.

## Neko Harbour

Topography
Neko Harbour is a small bay, with a cobble beach extending approx 500 metres at the southwestern end. Behind the beach a rocky outcrop leads up to the foot of a permanent snowslope. The glaciers around the site are highly crevassed and those surrounding the bay regularly cave.

Fauna
*Confirmed breeders:* Gentoo penguin (*Pygoscelis papua*), kelp gull (*Larus dominicanus*), and skuas (*Catharacta* spp.). *Regularly haul out:* Weddell seals (*Leptonychotes weddellii*).

Flora
Swards of moss species, the green alga *Prasiola crispa* and snow algae.

Other
There is an Argentine refuge hut on the site.

**Map 12. Neko Harbour, Andvord Bay**

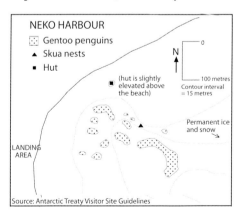

NEKO HARBOUR
⬚ Gentoo penguins
▲ Skua nests
■ Hut

N

(hut is slightly elevated above the beach)

0
100 metres
Contour interval = 15 metres

Permanent ice and snow

LANDING AREA

Source: Antarctic Treaty Visitor Site Guidelines

Visitor impact
*Known impacts:* None.
*Potential impacts:* Disturbance to wildlife.

Landing requirements
*Ships (A ship is defined as a vessel which carries more than 12 passengers.)*
• Ships carrying 500 or fewer passengers.
• One ship at a time.
• Maxiumum 3 ships per day (midnight to midnight), of which no more than two may be vessels carrying more than 200 passengers.

*Visitors*
• No more than 100 visitors ashore at any time, exclusive of expedition guides and leaders.
• 1 guide per 20 visitors.
• No visitors ashore between 22:00hrs and 04:00hrs (local time), except for those engaged in organised overnight stays. This is in order to establish a resting period for the wildlife.

Visitor area
*Landing area*
• On the cobble beach southwest of the refuge hut.

*Closed areas*
• None.

*Guided walking areas*
None

*Free roaming areas*
Visitors can roam freely, but under supervision.

Visitor Code of Conduct
*Behaviour ashore*
• Walk slowly and carefully.
• Maintain a precautionary distance of 5 metres from wildlife and give animals the right-of-way. Increase this distance if any change in behaviour is observed.
• Be careful near skuas, they may be aggressive.
• Do not walk on any vegetation.

*Cautionary notes*
• Be aware that glacier calving may produce dangerous waves.
• Avoid the beach or be prepared to evacuate quickly up the hill.
• Do not enter the refuge hut.

## Cuverville Island
Topography
This 2km by 2.5km island is a steep-sided dome, two-thirds of which is covered by a permanent ice-cap. The northern shore is a beach of cobbles and boulders, approx 1.5km long, backed by steep vegetation-covered cliffs toward the east and gentler slopes to the west.

Fauna
*Confirmed breeders:* Gentoo penguin (*Pygoscelis papua*), kelp gull (*Larus dominicanus*), Antarctic tern (Sterna vittata), snowy sheathbill (*Chionis alba*), blue-eyed shag (*Phalacrocorax atriceps*), Wilson's storm-petrel (*Oceanites oceanicus*), skuas (*Catharacta spp.*), snow petrel (*Pagodroma nivea*), pintado petrel (*Daption capense*).

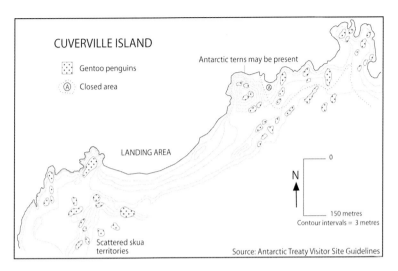

**Map 13. Cuverville Island, Errera Channel**

*Regularly haul out :* Weddell seals
*(Leptonychotes weddellii)* and Antarctic
fur seals *(Arctocephalus gazella)*. Leopard
seals *(Hydrurga leptonyx)* often hunt
near-shore.

Flora
*Deschampsia antarctica, Colobanthus
quitensis;* swards of moss species; and
lichen species including *Xanthoria* spp.,
*Buellia* spp., *Caloplaca* spp. *Usnea* spp.

Visitor impact
*Known impacts:* None.
*Potential impacts:* Disturbance of wildlife
and trampling of vegetation.

Landing requirements
*Ships (A ship is defined as a vessel which
carries more than 12 passengers.)*
• Ships carrying 500 or fewer passengers.

• One ship at a time.
• No more than 3 ships carrying more
than 200 passengers per day (midnight
to midnight).

*Visitors*
• No more than 100 visitors ashore at any
time, exclusive of expedition guides
and leaders.
• 1 guide per 20 visitors.
• No visitors ashore between 22:00hrs
and 04:00hrs (local time), except for
those engaged in organised overnight
stays. This is in order to establish a
resting period for the wildlife.

Visitor area
*Landing area*
• Primary: The wide cobble beach on
the northern end of the island. Avoid
landing in the immediate vicinity of

53

the gentoo colonies on the western end.
• Note: The small beaches on the eastern end of the site should not be used for landing, as they provide major access routes to the sea for penguins.

*Closed areas*
• Closed Area A: Small beaches where gentoo penguins access the sea.

*Guided walking areas*
None.

*Free roaming areas*
Visitors may roam freely, but under supervision, except in the closed areas. Visitors should always remain within the sight of guides.
Note: the eastern end of the island contains the same wildlife (gentoo penguins) as the west, but has less room for visitors, and a higher likelihood of disrupting routes to and from the sea. Therefore, guides should discourage visits to the eastern end.

Visitor Code of Conduct
*Behaviour ashore*
• Walk slowly and carefully.
• Maintain a precautionary distance of 5 metres from wildlife and give animals the right-of-way. Increase this distance if any change in behaviour is observed.
• Be careful near Antarctic fur seals and skuas, they may be aggressive. Do not walk on any vegetation.

*Cautionary notes*
• In the late season (moulting time), the density of penguins will probably confine visits to the immediate vicinity of the landing beach.

## Goudier Island and Port Lockroy 'Base A'
Topography
Goudier Island is a small low-lying rocky island. At the beginning of the season, fast ice is likely to surround much of it. Snow cover melts back during the summer.

Fauna
*Confirmed breeders:* Gentoo Penguins (*Pygoscelis papua*) and snowy sheathbills (*Chionis alba*). Dominican gulls (*Larus dominicanus*) and Subantarctic skuas (*Catharacta skua*) nest on the nearby Bills Island. Crabeater seals (*Lobodon carcinophagus*) also breed locally in Port Lockroy.
*Regularly haul out:* Weddell seals (*Leptonychotes weddelli*).

Flora
*Buellia* spp., and *Verrucaria* spp. are present. *Verrucaria serpuloides* (the only known marine lichen in the world) is restricted to this area, occurring from the low tide mark to ca. 10 metres depth. The green alga *Prasiola crispa* is frequent.

Other
'Base A' is designated as Historic Site and Monument No. 61 under the Antarctic Treaty. It is operated by the United

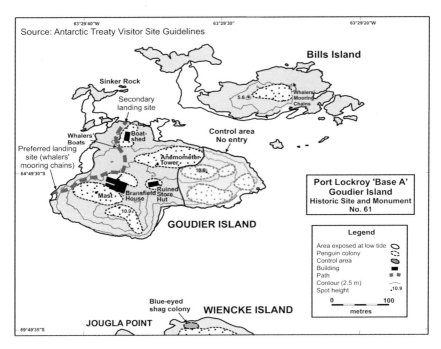

Map 14. Goudier Island, Port Lockroy

Kingdom as a living museum. In addition to Bransfield House (the main base building), there is a boat shed, building foundations and a number of associated artifacts on Goudier Island.

Visitor impact
*Known impacts:* The base staff monitor the population and breeding success of the gentoo penguins on the island. Despite high numbers of visitors, there has been no discernible impact on the breeding success of this colony.
*Potential impacts:* Fire. Minor fuel spills. Disturbance of wildlife and the monitoring programme.

Landing requirements
*Ships (A ship is defined as a vessel which carries more than 12 passengers.)*
• Ships carrying 500 or fewer passengers (however, note visitor restrictions below).
• One ship at a time.
• Maximum 3 ships per day (midnight to midnight).

*Visitors*
• No more than 60 visitors to the island at any time, exclusive of expedition guides and leaders.
• No more than 350 visitors per day.
• 1 guide to 20 visitors.

- 'Base A' and the associated artifacts on the island are owned and managed by the United Kingdom.
- Visits to the base may only take place with the prior agreement of the Base Leader (It is the UK's policy to only allow visits from Government or IAATO Member vessels. Visitors enter the base at their own risk and neither the British Antarctic Survey, the United Kingdom Heritage Trust, nor the UK authorities will be liable for any personal injury or damage to property that may be sustained.).
- No more than 35 visitors are allowed inside the base at any one time.
- Please respect the privacy of the occupants of the Base and do not land visitors ashore between 18:00hrs and 07:00hrs (local time), without express agreement from the Base Leader.
- Where practicable, Expedition Leaders are requested to invite at least one member of the Port Lockroy staff to come aboard the vessel to brief passengers and staff prior to any visit taking place.

Visitor area
*Landing area*
- The preferred site is on the west side of the island next to the whalers' mooring chains. When this is not accessible, an alternative is located on the north side of Goudier Island opposite the boat shed.

*Closed areas*
- The eastern side of the island is roped off and marked as an undisturbed.

*Guided walking areas*
None.

*Free roaming areas*
Visitors should use the two paths (shown on the map) which are maintained for access to and from the base. With the permission of the Base Leader, Visitors may also roam freely, but under close supervision, except in the closed areas. However, given the irregular topography at this site, guides should be aware that it is more difficult to ensure the necessary supervision of visitors.

Visitor Code of Conduct
*Behaviour ashore*
- Walk slowly and carefully.
- Give animals the right-of-way.
- Be aware that there is restricted visitor space on the island and particular caution should be exercised to avoid disturbing the wildlife.
- Be careful around the base buildings, structures and remains.
- Do not move or damage the whaling artefacts on the island.
- Before entering the base, all boots should be cleaned. As far as practicable, any snow or moisture from clothes and backpacks should be brushed off.
- Do not touch any artifacts on display, or any personal possessions of the staff who live at the base.
- Smoking is strictly prohibited.

*Cautionary notes*
- Be aware that this site can be particularly muddy, wet and slippery.

## Jougla Point on Wiencke Island

### Topography

Jougla Point is a rocky peninsula indented with small coves. At the beginning of the season fast ice is likely to surround the point. Snow cornices, glaciers and extensive, steep, and highly crevassed snowfields surround the harbour.

### Fauna

*Confirmed breeders:* Gentoo penguin (*Pygoscelis papua*) blue-eyed shag (*Phalacrocorax atriceps*), kelp gull (*Larus dominicanus*), Antarctic terns (*Sterna vittata*) and skuas (*Catharacta* spp.). *Regularly haul out:* Weddell seals (*Leptonychotes weddellii*)

### Flora

*Xanthoria* spp., *Caloplaca* spp., *Buellia* spp., other crustose lichen species, and the green alga *Prasiola crispa* are present but not widespread.

### Visitor impact

*Known impacts:* None.
*Potential impacts:* Disturbance of wildlife.

### Landing requirements

*Ships (A ship is defined as a vessel which carries more than 12 passengers.)*
• Ships carrying 500 or fewer passengers.
• One ship at a time.
• Maximum 3 ships per day (midnight to midnight).

**Map 15. Jougla Point, Wiencke Island**

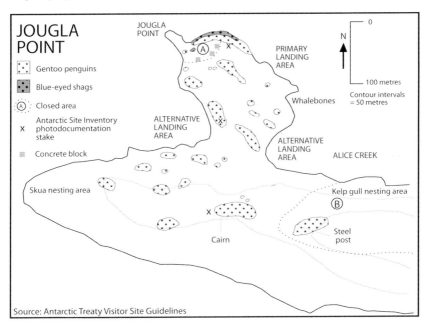

Source: Antarctic Treaty Visitor Site Guidelines

*Visitors*
- No more than 100 visitors at any time, exclusive of expedition guides and leaders.
- 1 guide to 20 visitors.
- No visitors ashore between 22:00hrs and 04:00hrs (local time), except for those engaged in organised overnight stays. This is in order to establish a resting period for the wildlife.

Visitor area
*Landing area*
- Primary area on boulders and rocks at the northeastern end of the Point.
- Alternative beaches on west side of the point or in Alice Creek on the east side of the Point (particularly suitable for small yachts).

*Closed areas*
- Closed Area A: Gentoo penguin and blue-eyed shag nesting area at the northwestern tip of Jougla Point behind the concrete blocks.
- Closed Area B: Higher rocky slope to the south of Alice Creek which includes a kelp gull colony.

*Guided walking areas*
None.

*Free roaming areas*
Visitors may roam freely, but under close supervision, except in the closed areas. Given the irregular topography at this site, guides should be aware that it is more difficult to ensure the necessary supervision of visitors.

Visitor Code of Conduct
*Behaviour ashore*
- Walk slowly and carefully.
- Maintain a precautionary distance of 5 metres from wildlife, and give animals the right-of-way. Increase this distance if any change in behaviour is observed.
- Be careful near Antarctic fur seals and skuas. They may be aggressive.
- Do not walk on any vegetation.

*Cautionary notes*
- Be aware that this site can be particularly muddy, wet and slippery.

## Pléneau Island
Topography
This island is around 1.2km long. From the cobbled beach on the eastern coast, smooth rock terraces slope gently upwards towards a large, potentially crevassed, ice-cap, which covers the western two-thirds of the island.

Fauna
*Confirmed breeders:* Gentoo penguins (*Pygoscelis papua*), kelp gulls (*Larus dominicanus*), south polar skuas (*Catharacta maccormicki*), and Antarctic terns (*Sterna vittata*).
*Haul out:* Southern elephant seals (*Mirounga leonina*).

Flora
Swards of moss species, *Caloplaca* spp. and other lichens, the green alga *Prasiola crispa* and snow algae.

Visitor impact
*Known impacts:* None.
*Potential impacts:* Disturbance of wildlife and trampling of vegetation.

Landing requirements
*Ships (A ship is defined as a vessel which carries more than 12 passengers.)*
• Ships carrying 200 or fewer passengers.
• One ship at a time.
• Maximum 3 ships per day (midnight to midnight).

*Visitors*
• No more than 100 visitors ashore at any time.
• 1 guide per 20 visitors.

**Map 16. Pléneau Island**

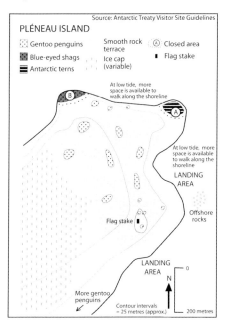

• No visitors ashore between 22:00hrs and 04:00hrs (local time), except for those engaged in organised overnight stays. This is in order to establish a resting period for the wildlife.

Visitor area
*Landing area*
• On rocks and boulders on the east-northeastern end, facing Booth Island.

*Closed areas*
• Closed Area A: Antarctic tern nesting area on the northeastern tip of the island.
• Closed Area B: Blue-eyed shag nesting area on the northern end of the island.

*Guided walking areas*
None.

*Free roaming areas*
Visitors may roam freely, but under close supervision, except in the closed areas. Given the irregular topography at this site, guides should be aware that it is more difficult to ensure the necessary supervision of visitors.

Visitor Code of Conduct
*Behaviour ashore*
• Walk slowly and carefully.
• Maintain a precautionary distance of 5 metres from wildlife and give animals the right-of-way. Increase this distance if any change in behaviour is observed.
• Be careful near skuas, they may be aggressive.
• Do not walk on any vegetation.

*Cautionary notes*
• Be sensitive to tern nesting sites, which may extend beyond the limits shown on the map for Closed Area A.

## Petermann Island
Topography
This 1km-long island rises up to approximately 150 metres above sea level. An ice-cap covers part of the northwestern end of the island and a potentially crevassed permanent ice-slope largely covers the southern end of the island. Many small cobbled bays indent its coastline, with nearly continuous rocky outcrops along the shore.

Fauna
*Confirmed breeders:* Adélie penguin (*Pygoscelis adeliae*), gentoo penguin (*Pygoscelis papua*), blue-eyed shag (*Phalacrocorax atriceps*), Wilson's storm petrel (*Oceanites oceanicus*), snowy sheathbill (*Chionis alba*), and south polar skua (*Catharacta maccormicki*).

Flora
*Deschampsia antarctica*; swards of moss species; *Xanthoria* spp., *Caloplaca* spp., and other crustose lichens; and the green alga *Prasiola crispa* are present. Snow algae may be extensive.

Other
• On the site there is an Argentine refuge hut.
• A commemorative cross and Historic Site and Monument No. 27 is also located on the site.

Visitor impact
*Known impacts:* None.
*Potential impacts:* Disturbance of wildlife and trampling of vegetation.

Landing requirements
*Ships (A ship is defined as a vessel which carries more than 12 passengers.)*
• Ships carrying 500 or fewer passengers.
• One ship at a time.
• Maximum 3 ships per day (midnight to midnight), of which no more than 2 may be vessels carrying more than 200 passengers.

*Visitors*
• No more than 100 visitors ashore at any time, exclusive of expedition guides and leaders.
• 1 guide per 20 visitors.
• No visitors ashore between 22:00hrs and 04:00hrs (local time), except for those engaged in organised overnight stays. This is in order to establish a resting period for the wildlife.

Visitor area
*Landing area*
• Along the shoreline in Port Circumcision.

*Closed areas*
• Closed Area A: Breeding Adélie penguins and blue-eyed shags in the vicinity of the basaltic dyke at the northeastern tip of the island.
• Closed Area B: Breeding Adélie

penguins at higher elevations northwest of Port Circumcision.

- Closed Area C: Southwestern end of the island, with breeding skuas, gentoo penguins and Wilson's storm petrels, and vegetation.

*Guided walking areas*
Visit to the Historic Site and Monument on Megalestris Hill or to the view point at the southern end of the island should be in guided groups.

*Free roaming areas*
Visitors may roam freely, but under close supervision, except in the closed or guided walking areas. Given the irregular topography at this site, guides should be aware that it is more difficult to ensure the necessary supervision of visitors. Note that the area north of Closed Areas A and B has less room for visitors, and a higher likelihood of disruption to the wildlife. Therefore, guides should discourage visits to this area.

**Map 17. Petermann Island, Penola Strait**

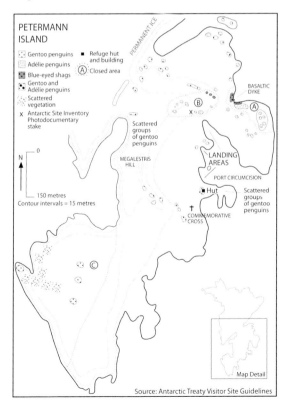

Source: Antarctic Treaty Visitor Site Guidelines

Visitor Code of Conduct
*Behaviour ashore*
- Walk slowly and carefully.
- Maintain a precautionary distance of 5 metres from wildlife and give animals the right-of-way. Increase this distance if any change in behaviour is observed.
- Be careful near skuas. They may be aggressive.
- Do not walk on any vegetation.

*Cautionary notes*
- Do not enter the refuge hut or damage, remove or destroy the designated Antarctic Historic Site and Monument, or the commemorative cross.
- Respect scientific and monitoring activities.

61

## Antarctic Specially Managed Areas

Entry into these areas does not require a special permit, but activities are subject to Codes of Conduct which are specific for each area. The ASMAs below are grouped by region and within each region are listed from north to south.

## South Shetland Islands

### Admiralty Bay at King George Island (ASMA No. 1)

This area comprises the terrestrial and marine area within the glacial drainage basin of Admiralty Bay (360 km²) (Map 18). It contains Arctowski Station (Poland), Comandante Ferraz Station (Brazil), Machu Picchu Station (Peru) and the summer field camps Refugio Ecuador (Ecuador) and Pieter J. Lenie (USA). ASPA No. 128 (Western shore of Admiralty Bay; access by Permit only) and HSM No. 51 (the grave of Wlodzimierz Puchalski near Arctowski Station) also lie within the area.

This ASMA was designated because of the area's "outstanding environmental, scientific, scenic and historic value, and the number of national Antarctic programmes and tourist parties operating in close proximity to one another". Site guidelines apply at the various stations and field camps, and visitors are requested to contact the station leaders as soon as possible on landing for a site briefing. A detailed management plan with maps has been agreed by the Treaty Parties, which

sets out a Code of Conduct, including preferred anchorages, and a number of zones to manage station activities and visitors and to protect important scientific and ecological sites. It is important to download and consult the plan prior to visiting (available from www.ats.aq/Atcm/RecAtt/Att338_e.pdf).

**Deception Island** (ASMA No. 4)

Deception Island (Map 19) is a unique Antarctic island with important natural, scientific, historic, educational, aesthetic and wilderness values. It has one of only two volcanoes in the Antarctic at which eruptions have been observed, and it is likely that there will be further eruptions in the future. The area has eight species of breeding seabirds and an exceptionally important flora, including at least 18 species that have not been recorded elsewhere in the Antarctic. Of particular importance are the very small, unique biological communities associated with the island's geothermal areas, and the most extensive known community of the flowering plant Antarctic pearlwort. The marine habitat of Port Foster is of ecological interest due to the natural perturbations caused by volcanic activity.

Note that the ASMA also includes ASPAs No. 140 and No. 145, and management of the island overall is achieved by a Management Package which aims to conserve and protect the unique environment, whilst managing the variety of competing demands placed upon it, including science, tourism, and the conservation of its natu-

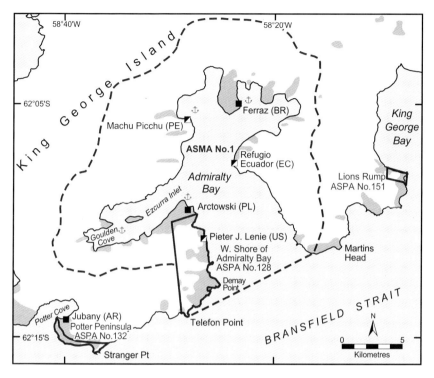

Map 18. Admiralty Bay, ASMA No. 1, King George Island

ral and historic values. It also aims to safeguard those working on, or visiting, the island. Strict Codes of Conduct apply.

There are three sites in particular that are frequently visited by cruise ships and yachts alike: Whalers Bay, Pendulum Cove and Baily Head. The first two have hot springs that are popular bathing spots. Visitors are requested not to scrape out swimming holes to sit in. When ashore at Whalers Bay, remain on the seaward side of the station ruins, the old waterboats and the piles of barrel

staves. When walking north of the station remains, do not go beyond the old airplane hangar in order to avoid entry into ASPA No. 140E. Do not enter buildings or sit on the boats. Approach oil and fuel tanks with caution, keeping in mind that the foundations are vulnerable to erosion and collapse of the tanks is possible. Be aware of the potential for flying debris in windy conditions.

Hikers visiting Neptune's Window should be careful to avoid areas of loose soil and scree around the lip of the Window to prevent erosion. Proceed along the beach in front of the waterboats, then up the slope towards the Window in single-file, using pre-existing tracks when visible. The return route should be the same.

Avoid traversing the scree slope towards the south where rockfalls are frequent.

Hikers visiting Baily Head should start their walk by following the drainage

**Map 19. Deception Island, ASMA No. 4**

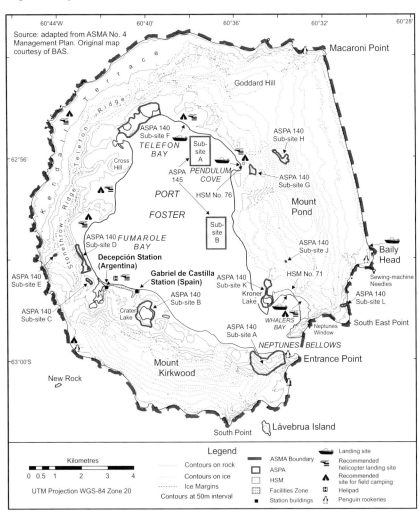

channels adjacent to Neptune's Window. Follow the drainage uphill but stay left and high during the ascent, and be aware that crevasses are opening up on the glacier. Once at the viewpoint of the outside of the caldera, continue northeastwards towards Baily Head, staying on the higher contour lines. When descending to the beach at Baily Head, take care not to disturb penguin-nesting activities.

This ASMA has its own website (www. deceptionisland.aq), from which you can download the management plan and codes of conduct that apply to visitor activities, the latest Deception Island news and, importantly, the island's current volcanic alert status.

## Antarctic Peninsula
### Southwest Anvers Island and Palmer Basin (proposed ASMA)

This area has a range of scientific and tourist activities associated principally with Palmer Station (US) (Maps 2 and 20). The proposed ASMA plan for this area contains codes of conduct and

Map 20. Palmer Station (US), Arthur Harbour, Anvers Island

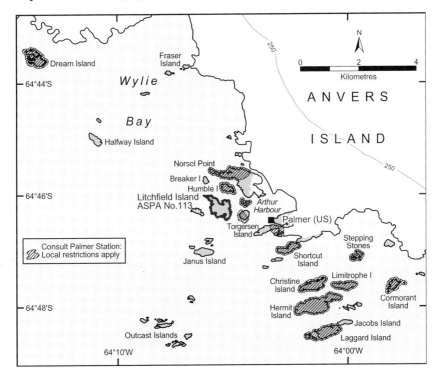

65

guidelines designed to help manage and protect local sites. They form the basis of locally accepted procedures for visits and operations in the vicinity of the station.

The proposed ASMA extends from the Rosenthal Islands south to the Joubin Islands and east to include the islands in

Arthur Harbour in the vicinity of Palmer Station, and would also include the Wauwermans, Dannebrog and Vedel Islands, which surround the Palmer Basin. This area has a wide range of important natural, scientific and educational visitor values. While at the time of writing the definitive ASMA plan has yet to be agreed, visitors should seek to observe the locally

Map 21. East Antarctica: permanent stations, specially managed and protected areas

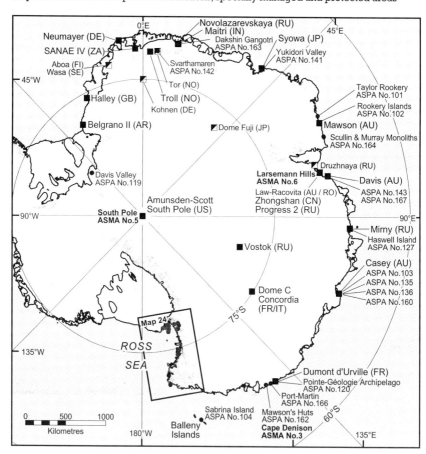

accepted procedures until such time as the new plan is adopted.

It is therefore important that you check the Antarctic Treaty website (www.ats. aq), ask your national authority, and when on-site consult with personnel at Palmer Station for the latest status and information. In the meantime, the main provisions of the proposed ASMA are outlined here. Of particular relevance to yachts and small boat operations are the various restrictions within the 'Visitor', 'Restricted' and 'Operations' zones that are proposed.

The proposed Operations Zone is a small area surrounding Palmer Station on Gamage Point. All visitors should contact Palmer Station at least 24 hours in advance of arrival to confirm details of the proposed visit. No more than 40 passengers are to be ashore at the station at any time.

Within the group of islands in Arthur Harbour, tourist landings should be confined to the Visitor Zone proposed on the northeast side of Torgersen Island. Landings on Torgersen Island should be made at the small boat landing site on the northern shore of the island (64°46'17.8"S, 64°04'31"W). No more than 40 passengers should be ashore at any time. The southern part of the island serves as an important scientific control site and is proposed as a Restricted Zone, so should be avoided (Map 20).

Within the proposed ASMA there are a number sites proposed as Restricted Zones, which are intended to limit access in order to protect on-going and long term ecological studies. Visitors should consult the Palmer Station manager to obtain the latest information on these sites and procedures to follow.

## East Antarctica (Map 21)

**Cape Denison** (ASMA No. 3) (Map 22) in Commonwealth Bay, George V Land, is one of the principal sites of early human activity in Antarctica, and holds important historical, cultural and scientific values. It is the location of the base of the Australasian Antarctic Expedition of

**Map 22. Cape Denison, ASMA No. 3, Commonwealth Bay**

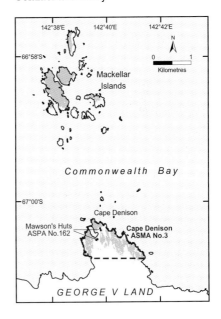

1911-14 organised and led by Douglas Mawson. It is one of only six hut sites remaining from this period and is an important symbol of the 'heroic age' of Antarctic exploration (1895-1917). The historic huts and immediate surrounds are further protected, being designated as ASPA No. 162, with some sections also designated as Historic Site and Monument No. 77.

Visits are permitted for the purpose of scientific research, historic conservation and archaeological work and for education or recreation including tourism. All land vehicles are prohibited within the area, with the exception of small all-terrain vehicles which, due to the colonisation of rocky areas by lichens and seabirds, should be used on snow and ice surfaces only, and with due consideration of the location of historic artefacts. Pedestrian access within the ASMA is unrestricted but artefact-rich areas (such as the scatter immediately to the north of the Main Hut), bird or lichen colonies, and penguin 'highways' (the established route of birds moving between their nest and the sea) should be avoided.

Visitors should not wash, swim or dive in the lakes. Tents should be pitched on the wooden platform adjacent to Sørensen Hut. Use of the huts and any supplies should be reported to the Australian national programme as soon as practicable to ensure the safety of other people who may be reliant upon known stores. No historic structure or other artefact should be damaged, destroyed or removed, unless removal of an artefact is essential for conservation purposes. Artefacts may only be removed by authorised personnel.

National programme personnel, tourists and other non-governmental personnel proposing to visit, land, and / or conduct activities in the area should inform the Australian national Antarctic programme (www.aad.gov.au) of their intentions as soon as is practicable. The details of all field activities should be accurately recorded for transfer to the management database of the Australian national programme.

**Larsemann Hills** (ASMA No. 6) (Map 23) is an ice-free area located on the south-eastern coast of Prydz Bay, Princess Elizabeth Land. Four research stations have been established on Broknes Peninsula at the east of the ASMA, including Law Base / Racovita (Australia / Romania), Zhongshan (China) and two Russian research stations (Progress I and Progress II). The purpose of the ASMA is primarily to assist in co-ordination of research programmes and associated infrastructure developments, and to protect important environmental values of the area. These values relate to the sensitive freshwater lakes and streams, landforms and the geology that are present. Although a few cruise ships have visited in recent years, sea ice conditions are frequently such that the site is generally not easily accessible by yachts. For example, most ships anchor up to 10 kilometres offshore, and sea ice

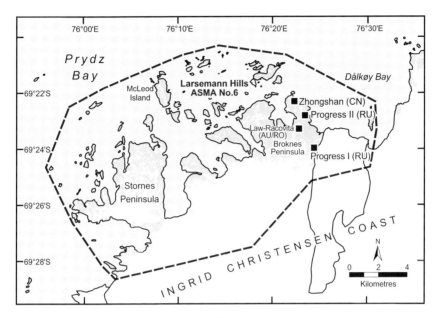

Map 23. Larsemann Hills, ASMA No. 6, Prydz Bay

debris can make access by small boat impossible, with helicopters often being the most practical means of access. Should it prove feasible to make a visit, you should be familiar with and observe the special requirements of the management plan, and visitors should liaise with station personnel before landing.

## The Ross Sea region (Map 24)

The McMurdo Dry Valleys (ASMA No. 2) (Map 25) in southern Victoria Land represent a nearly pristine cold desert ecosystem. The region has important scientific, aesthetic and wilderness values, with accumulated ice containing important records of past climate change, whilst the current climate serves as an important analogue for the conditions of ancient Earth and contemporary Mars. The area contains unusual microhabitats and biological communities, as well as special geological features and minerals (e.g. salt deposits and desert pavements). The principal activities within the Dry Valleys are science and its associated support services, and a US Long Term Ecological Research site has been established with a particular focus on Taylor Valley. Other activities include education, media and the arts, official national programme visitors, and tourism, all carried out according to the guidelines and Code of Conduct detailed in the management plan (www.ats.aq/Atcm/Rec Att/Att208_e.pdf).

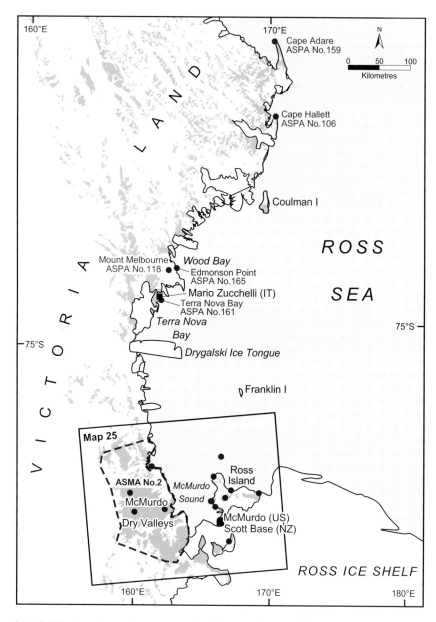

Map 24. The Ross Sea region: permanent stations and protected areas

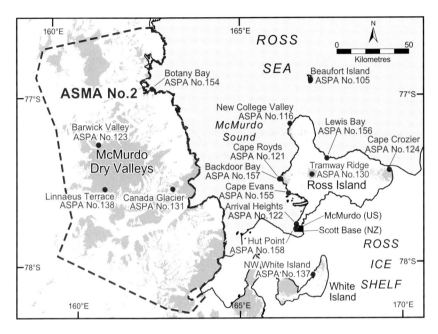

Map 25. The McMurdo Dry Valleys, Ross Island and protected areas

## Antarctic Specially Protected Areas

All Antarctic Specially Protected Areas (ASPAs) are 'out of bounds' for visitors unless a special permit for entry into a specific site has been issued by your responsible national authority. The ASPAs below are grouped by region and within each region are listed from north to south.

### South Orkney Islands (Map 26)

Northern Coronation Island (ASPA No. 114) is a representative example of the coastal, permanent ice and sub-littoral ecosystems typical of the maritime Antarctic environment.

Lynch Island (ASPA No. 110) has a loam-like soil with a rich invertebrate fauna, and is an outstanding example of a rare natural ecological system with one of the most extensive and dense stands of Antarctic hair grass known in the Antarctic.

Moe Island (ASPA No. 109) contains the largest continuous expanse of *Chorisodontium-Polytrichastrum* moss turf found in Antarctica. It is a representative example of the maritime Antarctic ecosystem and serves as an important control site for future comparisons with research sites on neighbouring Signy Island.

71

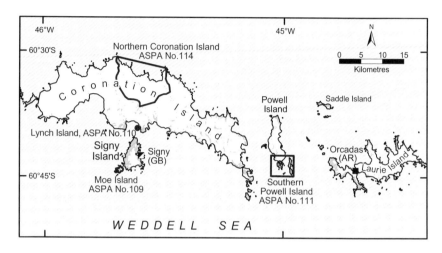

Map 26. The South Orkney Islands: permanent stations and protected areas

Southern Powell Island and adjacent islands (ASPA No. 111) (Map 27) support a diverse flora and fauna representative of the natural ecology of the South Orkney Islands. Anchoring in the area, including

Map 27. Southern Powell Island

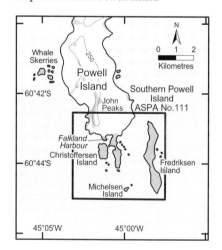

Falkland Harbour, should be avoided except in an emergency.

## South Shetland Islands
(Map 28)

Lions Rump (ASPA No. 151) (Map 18) is a representative example of a rich coastal ecosystem typical of King George Island, and is largely undisturbed by human activity.

Western shore of Admiralty Bay (ASPA No. 128) (Map 18), close to Arctowski Station on King George Island, contains an exceptional assemblage of seabirds and mammals. Long-term research programmes at the site could be jeopardised by accidental disturbance from visitors from the station and / or by tourists.

Potter Peninsula (ASPA No. 132) (Map 18) on King George Island has a diverse

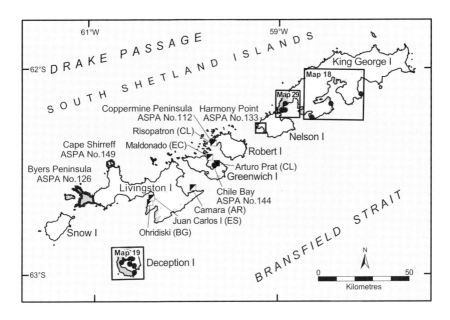

Map 28. The South Shetland Islands: permanent stations and protected areas

avian and mammal fauna and locally rich vegetation. Long-term research programmes on breeding populations of elephant seals and seabirds could be endangered by accidental disturbance, especially during breeding periods.

**Ardley Island** (ASPA No. 150) (Map 29) in Maxwell Bay, King George Island, has a diverse avifauna and a fellfield ecosystem dominated by macrolichens, which are sensitive to human disturbance.

**Fildes Peninsula** (ASPA No. 125) (Map 29) on King George Island consists of two sub-sites that contain unique fossil ichnolites which are vulnerable to souvenir collection by visitors.

Map 29. Maxwell Bay, King George Island: permanent stations and protected areas

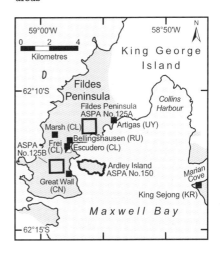

73

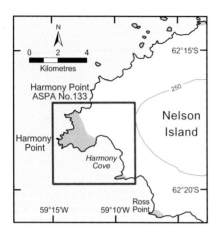

Map 30. Harmony Point, Nelson Island

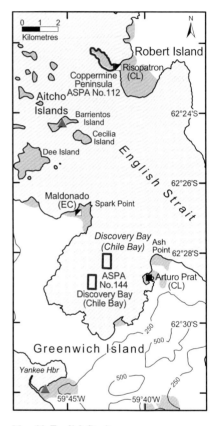

Map 31. English Strait area

**Harmony Point** (ASPA No. 133) (Map 30), Nelson Island, is an area with large breeding colonies of 11 seabird species and an abundance of vegetation which could be endangered by accidental disturbance.

**Coppermine Peninsula** (ASPA No. 112) (Map 31), Robert Island, is a biologically diverse area supporting one of the largest continuous moss stands in the Antarctic and a rich fauna.

**Chile Bay (Discovery Bay)** (ASPA No. 144) (Map 31), Greenwich Island, comprises two benthic research sites adjacent to Arturo Prat Station. Although ships may transit the area, bottom trawling should be avoided and anchoring should be avoided except in compelling circumstances.

**Cape Shirreff** (ASPA No. 149) (Map 32), Livingston Island, is an important site for marine ecosystem monitoring and supports an exceptional diversity of flora and fauna. The site is also of special archaeological importance.

**Byers Peninsula** (ASPA No. 126) (Map 33), Livingston Island, supports a diverse assemblage of flora and fauna and outstanding freshwater systems, which are sensitive to disturbance. It is also of exceptional historical interest, containing

Map 32. Cape Shirreff, Livingston Island

Map 33. Byers Peninsula, Livingston Island

the greatest concentration of 19th century historical sealing sites in Antarctica.

Map 34. Western Bransfield Strait

**Parts of Deception Island** (ASPA No. 140) (Map 19). This comprises 11 sub-sites distributed around the island, designated on the grounds that they are of exceptional scientific interest for the study of colonisation processes and are very vulnerable to disturbance. They are Collins Point (Site A), Crater Lake (Site B), Unnamed hill at southern end of Fumarole Bay (Site C), Fumarole Bay (Site D), West Stonethrow Ridge (Site E), Telefon Bay (Site F), Pendulum Cove (Site G), Mount Pond (Site H), 'Perchuc Cone' (Site J), Ronald Hill to Kroner Lake (Site K) and South East Point (Site L).

**Port Foster** (ASPA No. 145) (Map 19) at Deception Island consists of two small marine areas on the eastern side of the harbour which are of exceptional ecological interest because of their active volcanic character. Although ships may

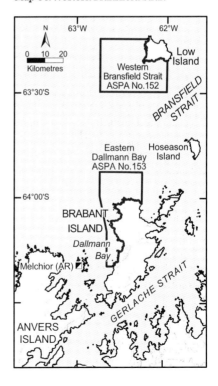

75

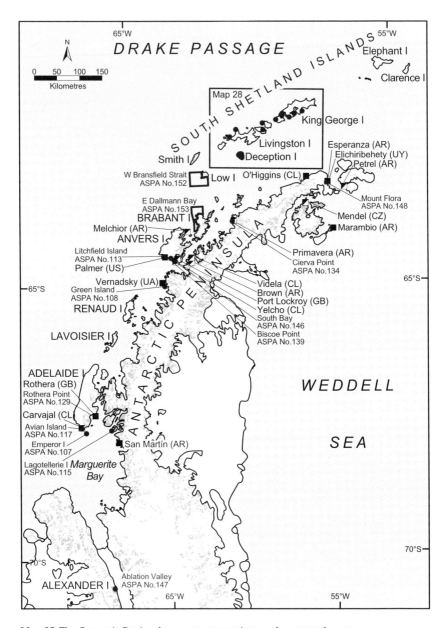

Map 35. The Antarctic Peninsula: permanent stations and protected areas

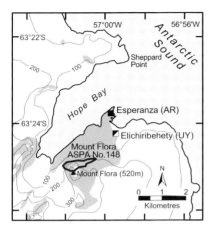

Map 36. Mount Flora, Hope Bay

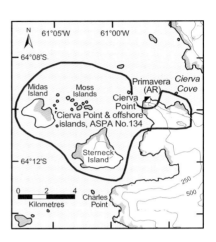

Map 37. Cierva Point

transit the area, bottom trawling should be avoided and anchoring should be avoided except in compelling circumstances.

**Western Bransfield Strait** (ASPA No. 152) (Map 34) off Low Island is designated to protect scientific studies of marine communities. Although ships may transit the area, bottom trawling should be avoided. Anchoring should also be avoided except in compelling circumstances.

### Antarctic Peninsula (Map 35)

**Mount Flora** (ASPA No. 148) (Map 36), Hope Bay, has important fossiliferous strata which require protection from souvenir collection by visitors and over-sampling by scientific programmes.

**Cierva Point** and adjacent offshore islands (ASPA No. 134) (Map 37) in Hughes Bay are sites of long-term research programmes with a diverse flora and fauna.

**Eastern Dallmann Bay** (ASPA No. 153) (Map 34) includes the shallow marine shelf area down to 200 m depth to the west and north of Brabant Island. The area is designated to protect scientific studies of the marine communities. Although ships may transit the area, bottom trawling should be avoided. Anchoring should also be avoided except in compelling circumstances.

**South Bay** (ASPA No. 146) (Map 38) at Doumer Island is a long-term research site for marine ecology. Ships may transit though the area, although anchoring should be avoided except in an emergency.

**Biscoe Point** (ASPA No. 139) (Map 39) on Anvers Island contains a large stand of the two native flowering plants and several long-term seabird research sites that are vulnerable to disturbance from scientific personnel or from tourist groups.

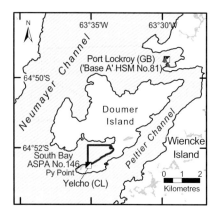

Map 38. Doumer Island

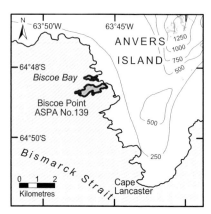

Map 39. Biscoe Point, Anvers Island

Litchfield Island (ASPA No. 113) (Map 20) possesses an unusually rich assemblage of marine and terrestrial life and provides an outstanding example of the natural ecological system of the Antarctic Peninsula area.

Green Island (ASPA No. 108) (Map 40) in the Berthelot Islands has exceptionally rich vegetation, with well-developed continuous banks of moss turf and areas of peat more than 1 m in depth.

Rothera Point (ASPA No. 129) (Map 41) on Adelaide Island is a long-term research site for monitoring the impact of nearby Rothera station (UK) on an Antarctic fellfield ecosystem.

Avian Island (ASPA No. 117) (Map 42) consists of the island together with its littoral zone and the marine area within 100 m of the shore. It is designated on the grounds that it is unique in the Antarctic

Peninsula region for its abundance and diversity of breeding seabirds.

Emperor Island (ASPA No. 107) (Map 42), Dion Islands, includes Emperor Island and the sea within 1 km of the coast. The island hosts the only colony of emperor penguins known to breed on the western side of the Antarctic Peninsula and is one of only two at which breeding occurs on land. Summer visits by boat to view the birds from offshore will be unrewarded since the penguins arrive at the island in late April and depart in November.

Lagotellerie Island (ASPA No. 115) (Map 43) contains a relatively diverse fauna typical of the southern Antarctic Peninsula, and one of the largest stands of Antarctic hair grass and Antarctic pearlwort known south of the South Shetland Islands.

Ablation Valley-Ganymede Heights (ASPA No. 147) (Map 35) in the interior of King

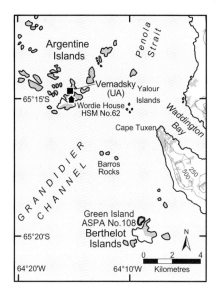

Map 40. Green Island, Berthelot Islands

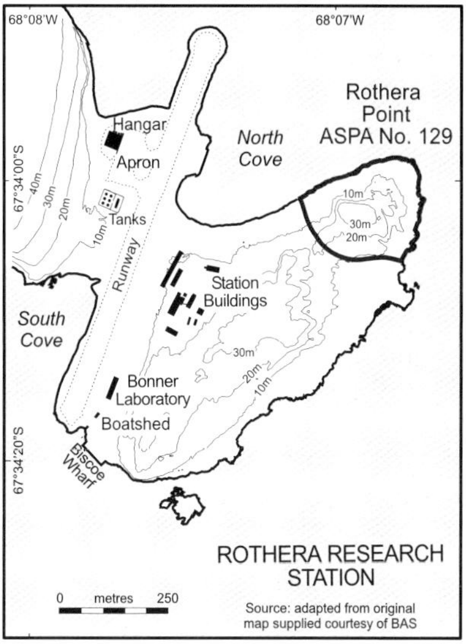

Map 41. Rothera Point, Adelaide Island

Map 42. Avian Island, Marguerite Bay

Map 43. Lagotellerie Island, Marguerite Bay

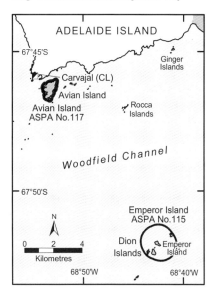

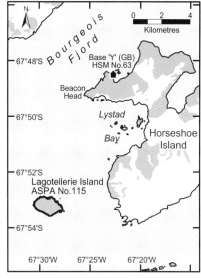

George VI Sound at the southern end of Marguerite Bay represents one of the largest ablation areas in West Antarctica and has important biological and geomorphological values.

## West Antarctica (from 45°E –0°E)

Davis Valley and Forlidas Pond (ASPA No. 119) (Map 21) in the Dufek Massif have exceptional geomorphological, freshwater and biological values.

## East Antarctica (from 0°E – 155°E) (Map 21)

Svarthamaren (ASPA No. 142) (Map 21) is the breeding locality of the largest known Antarctic petrel colony on the Antarctic continent.

Dakshin Gangotri Glacier (ASPA No. 163) (Map 21) has unique scientific and biological values.

Yukidori Valley (ASPA No. 141) (Map 21) is representative of the typical Antarctic fellfield ecosystem and the subject of long-term biological research and monitoring.

Taylor Rookery (ASPA No. 101) (Map 44) is the site of a large emperor penguin colony, one of the few and probably the largest colony of emperor penguins located entirely on land.

Rookery Islands (ASPA No. 102) (Map 44) contain an unusual association of six bird species including southern giant petrels and cape petrels.

Scullin and Murray Monoliths (ASPA No. 164) (Map 45), Mac.Robertson Land hold the greatest concentration of breeding seabird colonies in Greater Antarctica, and notably the second largest colony of Antarctic petrels.

Map 44. Taylor Rookery and Rookery Islands

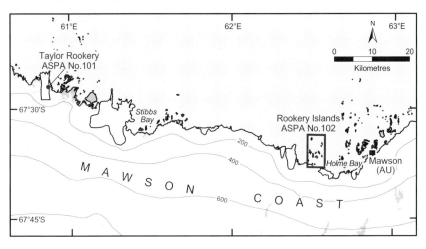

**Marine Plain** (ASPA No. 143) (Map 46) contains vertebrate fossil fauna, including a recently discovered fossil dolphin.

**Hawker Island** (ASPA No. 167) (Map 46) lies approximately 300 m offshore on the Ingrid Christensen Coast, Princess Elizabeth Land, and is designated to prevent human disturbance to the southernmost colony of southern giant petrels on continental Antarctica.

**Haswell Island** (ASPA No. 127) (Map 47) is an important and representative breeding locality for seabird species in this part of the Antarctic, including emperor penguins. It offers exceptional opportunities for research and needs protection in view of its close proximity to a large research station.

**Ardery Island and Odbert Island** (ASPA No. 103) (Map 48) support populations

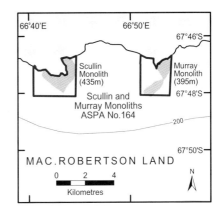

Map 45. Scullin and Murray Monoliths

of Antarctic petrel, Antarctic fulmar, cape petrel, and Wilson's storm-petrel in typical breeding habitat.

**Northeastern Bailey Peninsula** (ASPA No. 135) (Map 48) contains contrasting habitats and water bodies, has extremely rich lichen

Map 46. Marine Plain and Hawker Island

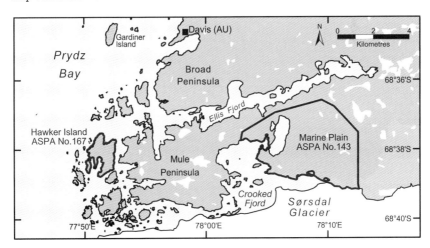

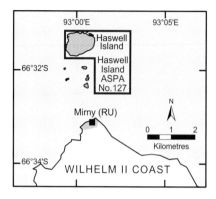

Map 47. Haswell Island

and moss communities and an important stand of liverwort. Protection is required to ensure study areas are not disturbed, and the boundary is prominently marked.

**Clark Peninsula** (ASPA No. 136) (Map 48) contains moss and lichen communities that are being used as control sites to monitor the environmental impact of nearby Casey Station.

**Frazier Islands** (ASPA No. 160) (Map 48) is the site of one of only four known breeding localities of southern giant petrels around the coastline of continental Antarctica, and as such is a reference area for comparative studies with other breeding populations of this species.

**Pointe-Géologie Archipelago** (ASPA No. 120) (Map 49) is a representative area of considerable biological, geological and aesthetic value, which contains a high diversity of flora and fauna and is an important area for scientific research.

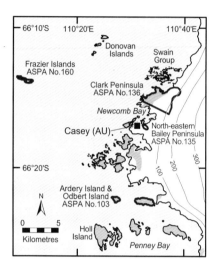

Map 48. Ardery Island and Odbert Island, Northeastern Bailey Peninsula, Clark Peninsula, and Frazier Islands

**Port-Martin** (ASPA No. 166) (Map 21), Terre Adélie, comprises the buildings and installations of Port-Martin Base constructed in 1950 by the 3rd French expedition and partly destroyed by fire in 1952.

**Mawson's Huts** (ASPA No. 162) (Map 22) comprises the four huts from the Australasian Antarctic Expedition of 1911-14 and a 5 m buffer zone extending from the perimeter of each hut.

## The Ross Sea region
(Map 24)

**Sabrina Island** (ASPA No. 104) (Map 50) supports a representative sample of the flora and fauna typical of the Balleny Islands, which reflects the circumpolar distributions of various species at this latitude.

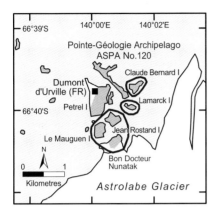

Map 49. Pointe-Géologie Archipelago

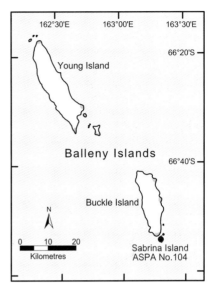

Map 50. Sabrina Island, Balleny Islands

**Cape Adare** (ASPA No. 159) (Map 24) is an important symbol of the Heroic Age of Antarctic exploration. Two of the three huts here were built in 1899 by Borchgrevink's British Antarctic Expedition (1898-1900), and used for the first winter spent on the Antarctic continent. The third hut was built by Scott's British Antarctic Expedition (1910-13) Northern Party, which wintered here in 1911.

**Cape Hallett** (ASPA No. 106) (Map 51) is one of only a few relatively accessible sites of high aesthetic, wildlife, and historical value in the northern Ross Sea. The site is also of high scientific value because of the large penguin colony, areas richly colonised by vegetation, and for studies of past ecosystem disturbance and recovery. Tourist visits are allowed by Permit within a Managed Zone, which comprises the site of the former Hallett Station (NZ/US) and an area along the shoreline of Seabee Hook.

**Summit of Mt Melbourne** (ASPA No. 118) (Map 52) possesses ice-free geothermal areas with unique moss and liverwort communities.

Map 51. Cape Hallett

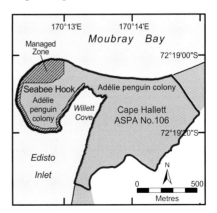

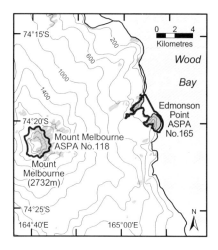

**Map 52. Mt Melbourne and Edmonson Point**

**Edmonson Point** (ASPA No. 165) (Map 52) is a small coastal ice-free area at the foot of Mount Melbourne with outstanding ecological and scientific values (terrestrial and freshwater ecosystems, and ongoing research on Adélie penguins) which require protection from possible interference that might arise from unregulated access.

**Terra Nova Bay** (ASPA No. No. 161) (Map 53) is a coastal marine area between Adélie Cove and Tethys Bay with an important and diverse littoral area that is valuable for long-term scientific studies being carried out from nearby Mario Zucchelli Station (Italy). Anchoring is prohibited within the area.

**Botany Bay** (ASPA No. 154) (Map 25) is an extremely rich high latitude botanical refuge with a lichen and moss species

diversity and abundance that is unique for southern Victoria Land.

**Barwick Valley** (ASPA No. 123) (Map 25) is one of the least disturbed and contaminated of the McMurdo Dry Valleys (ASMA No. 2), and is strictly protected as a reference area.

**Linnaeus Terrace** (ASPA No. 138) (Map 25) is located in the Upper Wright Valley and is protected as one of the richest localities where unique cryptoendolithic communities are found and for its fragile weathered rock formations.

**Canada Glacier** (ASPA No. 131) (Map 25) in the Taylor Valley contains some of the richest growths of algae and mosses in the McMurdo Dry Valleys, and is a valuable reference site for other dry

**Map 53. Terra Nova Bay**

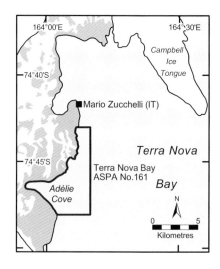

valley ecosystems. The concentration of research activity within the area makes it necessary to regulate human impact with respect to trampling, water quality and sampling.

**Beaufort Island** (ASPA No. 105) (Map 25) is one of the most important seabird breeding areas in the Ross Sea and has the most extensive, continuous area of mosses known in the McMurdo Sound region, with a natural ecological system that should be preserved as a reference area.

**Cape Crozier** (ASPA No. 124) (Map 25) is a site of long-term penguin studies that require protection from disturbance by visitors.

**Lewis Bay** (ASPA No. 156) (Map 25) is the site where an Air New Zealand DC-10 aircraft crashed into the northern slope of Mount Erebus on 28 November 1979, killing all 257 people on board. The area is strictly protected as a mark of respect and in order to leave the area in peace.

**Tramway Ridge** (ASPA No. 130) (Map 25) has unusual vegetation associated with geothermal and fumarolic activity near the summit of Mount Erebus.

**New College Valley** (ASPA No. 116) (Map 25) at Cape Bird, Ross Island, supports stands of moss, algae, and lichens which are amongst the most extensive and luxuriant in southern Victoria Land and the subject of long-term research.

**Cape Royds** (ASPA No. 121) (Map 25) contains the world's most southerly known Adélie penguin colony. The marine area protects the seaward access and inshore feeding ground of the penguins, as well as existing and projected research on the marine ecosystem.

**Backdoor Bay** (ASPA No. 157) (Map 25) is the site of the historic hut built by Sir Ernest Shackleton's British Antarctic (*Nimrod*) Expedition (1907-09), and is one of the principal sites of the Heroic Age of Antarctic exploration.

**Cape Evans** (ASPA No. 155) (Map 25) is the site of the hut built in 1911 by Robert Falcon Scott's Terra Nova Expedition (1910-13), and is one of the principal sites of the Heroic Age of Antarctic exploration.

**Hut Point** (ASPA No. 158) (Map 25) is the site of the hut built in 1902 by Robert Falcon Scott's British National Antarctic (*Discovery*) Expedition of 1901-04.

**Arrival Heights** (ASPA No. 122) (Map 25) has high scientific value for a variety of long-term atmospheric programmes, for which sensitive instrumentation requires interference to kept to the minimum practicable.

**Northwest White Island** (ASPA No. 137) (Map 25) contains the most southerly known colony of Weddell seals, which is also unusual because it is physically isolated from the open sea by enclosing ice shelves.

# Southern Ocean Islands North of 60°S

The Southern Ocean and sub-Antarctic islands listed in this section lie north of the Antarctic Treaty area, i.e. north of 60°S, and their administration is the responsibility of their respective governments. However, the same principles of environmental protection for the Antarctic Treaty area also apply at most of these islands. Documents (passport, ship's papers etc) may be required at those islands where government officials are posted. Laws and regulations relating to conservation and visitors vary according to each government's ordinances and are enforced by law. Additional or more stringent conditions may apply at some islands and the relevant government agency(ies) should be contacted well before departure to confirm specific requirements.

The *IAATO Marine Wildlife Watching Guidelines* (Annex III, p. 118) and *Decontamination Guidelines* (Annex IV, p.123) are essential reference documents for environmental protection when visiting Southern Ocean islands, and they should be consulted in conjunction with any local regulations in force.

## Tierra del Fuego

This vast archipelago lies at the southern tip of South America between the Pacific and Atlantic Oceans (Map 54). It comprises all those islands south of the Estrecho de Magallanes (Straits of Magellan) to Cabo de Hornos (Cape Horn).

The eastern half of the largest island (Isla Grande) and Isla de los Estados (Staten Island) are governed by Argentina, while the remaining area to the west and all other islands, including Islas Diego Ramirez and Ildefonso to the south in Drake Passage, fall under Chilean jurisdiction as part of the Region Magallanes. With the exception of Isla Grande, Isla Navarino and a few smaller adjacent islands, Tierra del Fuego is virtually uninhabited. The total population is 120,000 and most people live in the principal towns of Porvenir and Puerto Williams (Chile) and Rio Grande and Ushuaia (Argentina). The Chilean town of Punta Arenas lies on the northern side of the Straits of Magellan and is not, strictly speaking, in Tierra del Fuego. It is the seat of the Chilean territorial government for the Region Magallanes and one of the principal ports of entry to the Chilean Fuegian Channels. The Argentine territorial government is in Ushuaia. Outside these four main towns, the population is made up of isolated communities living on the large estancias (sheep farms) on Isla Grande, and a few farming families on Islas Navarino and Hoste. The area west of Ushuaia is virtually uninhabited, except for the occasional fishermens' camp and Chilean military personnel stationed

Map 54. Tierra del Fuego: main settlements and protected areas

at a number of observation posts along the Channels.

If you arrive in Tierra del Fuego through the Estrecho de Magallanes (Straits of Magellan), either from the Pacific or Atlantic Ocean, your first port of entry must be Punta Arenas. If you arrive from the Atlantic via the Estrecho de Lemaire (Lemaire Strait) and the Canal Beagle (Beagle Channel), your first port of entry can be Ushuaia (providing you do not cross into Chilean waters on the way in) or Puerto Williams (Chile). If you wish to enter after rounding Cabo de Hornos (Cape Horn), you must proceed to Puerto Williams via the east coast of Isla Navarino. On no account must the Canal Murray be used. This area is open only to Chilean flagged vessels and

if you inadvertently enter the channel, you will be stopped by the Chilean navy and escorted to Puerto Williams. Isla de los Estados is closed to all visitors except the Argentine Navy and scientists, although a permit to visit may be granted on request to authorities at Recursos Naturales in Ushuaia, and vessels are permitted to shelter on passage if weather or other conditions are unfavourable. In June 2005, the Chilean region of Tierra del Fuego south of the Cordillera Darwin was declared a Biosphere Reserve, the 'Cape Horn Biosphere Reserve', by UNESCO, designated on account of its extremely rich biodiversity.

You need a 'zarpe' (an official authorisation or navigation permit) to cruise in the Chilean Fuegian Channels. A 'zarpe' can be arranged through the Chilean Consulate of any country, or it can be done by the Harbourmaster ('Capitania de Puerto') in a matter of a few hours on arrival at your port of entry. A 'zarpe' is valid for a maximum of 90 days (maximum tourist stay) and can be renewed for another 90 days after payment of US$100.Customs entry for the vessel is 120 days and this can also be renewed.

When entering Chile for the first time, be sure to establish radio contact as you pass the observation posts (for example at the entrance to the Straits of Magellan, on Cape Horn and in the Beagle Channel), giving name of vessel, number of crew aboard, last port of call and destination. Entry formalities are carried out by officials from Customs, the Harbourmaster, Ministry of Agriculture and Immigration. A fee is charged according to vessel tonnage for entering and leaving Chile. An extra fee applies for out of office hours. Vessels must also pay a contribution to the maintenance of lights and signals (faros y balizas) – in the Channels. At Punta Arenas, yachts usually anchor on the south side of the jetty, and the skipper will have to go ashore to contact the authorities after advising them of your arrival on VHF by calling 'Capuerto Punta Arenas'. At Puerto Williams, yachts may tie up at the Club de Yates Micalvi alongside the vessel *Micalvi* (fees apply), where officials will board upon arrival – call 'Capuerto Williams' on VHF.

Shipping in the Chilean Channels is restricted to the commercial navigation route marked on the marine charts. If you wish to sail outside this route, permission *must* be obtained from the Chilean authorities. When completing departure formalities at Puerto Williams or Punta Arenas, discuss your intended route with the Harbourmaster who will advise you as to which Channels can be visited and which ones are out of bounds. It is recommended that you stick to this route as the Channels are well patrolled by the Chilean Navy and maritime traffic control and observation posts. You are required to signal your position daily to Chilean authorities on VHF Channel 16, reporting either to military vessels or observation posts in your vicinity. If you don't have a VHF radio, you will be required to purchase one before being issued with your 'zarpe'.

No navigation permit is necessary in Argentine waters. All entry and departure formalities are done at the local Prefectura in Ushuaia (Ushuaia Prefectura Naval, Calle Yaghanes 59). Officials maintain a listening watch on VHF Channels 12 and 16, call sign L3P ('Lima Tres Papa Prefectura Naval Ushuaia'). Customs officials (Aduana Ushuaia) are stationed at the commercial jetty (Muelle Comercial). On arrival at Ushuaia, you may tie up at the Afasyn Yacht Club jetty (fees apply) while the entry formalities are being completed. There is no customs fee if entry formalities are completed during working hours but a fee is charged for after-hours or weekends.

Once the clearance is ready, you can move to the Club Nautico (no fee), or anchor or take up a mooring (fees apply).

While in port, garbage may be disposed of at the local yacht clubs or in the public garbage cans. When cruising the Channels, store all non-biodegradables on board until back in port.

If you intend sailing direct to the Antarctic Peninsula from Chile or Argentina, you are not required to do customs clearance providing you intend to return direct to Chile or Argentina at the end of your cruise. This is because both countries consider the Antarctic to be a part of their respective countries. If heading north, you will have to clear customs and immigration at the Prefectura Naval in Ushuaia, or the Capitania de Puerto in Puerto Williams or Punta Arenas. If you clear from Puerto Williams for Antarctica, and you will be issued with a 'zarpe' which is effectively a permit to sail in Chilean Antarctic waters and you will be required to report to Chilean vessels and stations while in the Antarctic. Failure to do so may result in a fine. If clearing from Ushuaia you must take care not to enter Chilean territorial waters on the way out: remain on the north side of the Beagle Channel until well east of Islas Lennox, Picton and Nueva. If you enter Chilean waters while in the vicinity of Chilean observation posts on these islands and without having cleared from Puerto Williams, you may be obliged to turn back, and if you eventually return to the area at a later date, you may

have to account for your failure to clear with the Chilean authorities.

Although most of the islands in Tierra del Fuego are government owned, there is some privately-owned land, mainly on Isla Grande. Here, permission should be sought from the landowner before setting off on hikes. Estancias are not open to the public: visits are upon invitation only. If you open gates, be sure to close them, and cross fences by passing between the wires, or at posts, to avoid damaging the fence. Isla de los Estados is an Argentine Provincial Reserve and special permission is required to visit, although vessels are allowed to anchor to wait on improvements in the weather when transiting Lemaire Strait.

Hunting and fishing are controlled by law in Argentina, a licence being necessary, as well as permission from the landowner. The fishing season (line-fishing for trout and salmon) is from 1 October – 31 March. The season for centollas (king crab) is from 1 December to 1 April. The only animals considered a real pest or abundant enough to shoot are upland geese, rabbits, beavers and muskrats. Protected animals include guanaco, nutria (coipu), all marine mammals (whales, dolphins, seals, otters), penguins, swans, rheas (nandus), curlews and knots (chorlos), snipe (becasina), condors, torrent ducks, kingfishers, all eagles, hawks, falcons, all ducks, the white form of the upland goose, ruddy-headed goose, and lizards.

In Chile, protected animals include the Patagonian fox, all marine mammals, otters, guanaco, swans, hawks, white owl, flamingos, ostrich (nandu), torrent duck, herons, penguins, kingfisher, and doves.

In the past, Tierra del Fuego was inhabited by nomadic Indian tribes. All archaeological and historic sites are protected. A permit is necessary for scientific expeditions intending to excavate sites. No relics, fossils, or artefacts may be removed without government permission. If you find an Indian campsite, do not disturb the ground or remove relics.

On no account should mussels, 'cholgas' or any other shellfish be eaten in the Channels. They may be toxic due to the effect of 'red tide' (marea roja), which causes death within 24 hours. Because of this, the Chilean 'zarpe' states that harvesting, cooking and eating of any kind of shellfish is prohibited.

*Visit enquiries*
Ushuaia Tourist Information Office, San Martin 674, Ushuaia.
Oficina Antartica at the 'Muelle Comercial', Ushuaia. Tel: +54 2901 430015.
Punta Arenas Tourist Office, Sernatur, Waldo Seguel 689, Punta Arenas.
Instituto Antártico Chileno, Plaza Muñoz Gamero 1051, Punta Arenas. Tel: +56 61298100.

*Publications*
Goodall, R.N.P. (1970) *Tierra del Fuego.* Ediciones Shanamaiim, Buenos Aires.

Mariolina Rolfo and Giorgio Ardrizzi. (2004) Patagonia & Tierra del Fuego Nautical Guide. Editrice Incontri Nautici, Rome.
Foucard, M. (1995) Terres Australes: Péninsule Antarctique et Terre de Feu. GNGL-DMI, Torcy.

*Websites*
Instituto Antártico Chileno: www.inach.cl
Instituto Antártico Argentino: www.dna.gov.ar
www.capehorn-pilot.com

## South Atlantic islands

Islands of the South Atlantic include South Georgia, the South Sandwich Islands, the Falkland Islands and Gough Island. Sovereignty of the island groups of the Falklands, South Georgia and South Sandwich Islands is claimed by both the United Kingdom and Argentina.

### The Falkland Islands
The Falkland Islands archipelago (Map 55) comprises over 700 islands and lies approximately 600 km northeast of Cape Horn near the tip of South America. It is inhabited by 3000 people of mainly British descent whose occupation of the islands dates back to the first permanent British settlement in 1833. Two thousand people live in the capital Stanley and the remainder in rural areas (locally known as camp) on the 88, mostly privately owned, sheep farms of East and West Falklands and small offshore islands.

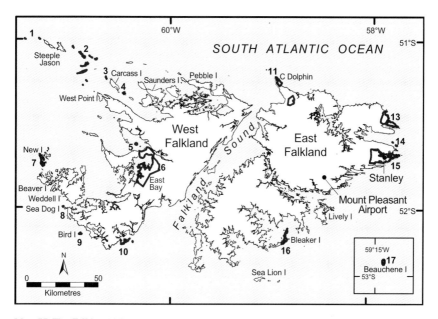

Map 55. The Falkland Islands: main settlements and National Nature Reserves

1. Jason East Cay, Jason West Cay and adjacent islets; 2. Flat Jason Island, Elephant Jason Island, South Jason Island, North Fur Island, South Fur Island, The Fridays, White Rock and adjacent islets. 3. The Twins; 4.Low Island; 5. Middle Island; 6.East Bay.; 7.New Island South; 8. Sea Dog; 9. Bird Island; 10. Peat Island and Arch Islands and adjacent islets; 11. Cape Dolphin; 12. Moss Side; 13. Volunteer Point and Cow Bay area; 14. Kidney Island and Cochon Island; 15. Stanley Common and Cape Pembroke; 16. Bleaker Island (North); 17. Beauchene Island

The Falkland Islands are a self-governing UK Overseas Territory, administered by the civil service of the Falkland Islands Government and its elected Councillors, in accordance with legislation and the 1985 Falklands Islands Constitution, under the overall authority of a Governor appointed by HM The Queen. A military garrison (1500 people) at Mount Pleasant Complex further defends the British claim to the islands.

Yachts are required to make Stanley their first port of entry. It is recommended that you provide your estimated date of arrival at least 24 hours in advance to the Customs and Immigration Department by faxing or emailing, or alternatively call the Harbour Authorities (call sign 'Fishops' or 'Stanley Port Control') on HF radio 4066.1 KHz.

All vessels, both on arrival and departure, are required to report to the Harbour

Authorities on VHF Channel 16 or 10 (24 hour listening watch, and HF 4066.1 KHz and 2182 KHz during office hours) on crossing the designated 'Reporting Line' that runs from Cape Pembroke to Volunteer Point. In case of emergencies, a 24 hour listening watch is also maintained by Stanley Police (call sign 'Stanley Police') on VHF 16. Vessels entering Stanley Harbour should also advise the Harbour Authorities of their estimated entry time at The Narrows, and request permission to berth or anchor. If no prior arrangements have been made for a berth at one of the available jetties, yachts should anchor off the Public Jetty and request customs clearance by calling Customs (call sign 'Customs') on VHF 16 or 12, or the Harbour Authorities or Stanley Police.

Harbour dues and customs fees apply to all yachts: at the time of writing, those on a private cruise with no paying passengers and under 50 tons, are charged a total of £60; if over 50 tons, the charges total £216.40 in office hours, and £280.60 out of office hours. Commercial yachts i.e. with paying passengers, under 50 tons are charged £172.40 in office hours and £236.60 out of office hours. Commercial yachts over 50 tons are also charged £300 harbour dues on the first day and £150 per day thereafter for the duration of their stay. A complimentary copy of the Falkland Islands Ports and Harbour Information booklet is available from the Customs Officer on entry. Permission should always be sought from the Harbour Authorities by VHF 16 or 10 before leaving a berth or

anchorage in Stanley Harbour. All vessels at anchor within Falklands harbours should keep a good listening watch on VHF 16.

Prolongation of your stay in the Islands is at the discretion of the Customs and Immigration Department. Note that it is a requirement for all visitors to the Falkland Islands to possess a medical / travel insurance policy which includes provision for emergency aero-medical evacuation to a third country, e.g. Chile or Uruguay.

The Falkland Islands are virtually free of any serious animal diseases and there are very strict laws relating to the importation of plants and animals: no live animals, animal products, plants or plant products can be brought ashore. All pets must remain on board and a yacht carrying pets must not tie up to any jetty. Clothing and footwear must be clean and free of soil. Any queries should be addressed to the Department of Agriculture. During your stay, you will be required to store all galley waste in garbage disposal bags provided by Customs and Immigration who will arrange to collect them before you leave. This is to minimise the risk of spreading Foot and Mouth Disease. Other wastes may be bagged and disposed of in public rubbish bins.

Yachts may berth on the east side of the public jetty (with permission from the Harbour Authorities) to obtain Customs clearance and for short stays, provided the facility is not in use by tenders from visiting cruise ships – cruise ship dates are posted on www.sulivanshipping.com. Berths (charges apply) are also available at the commercial floating jetty (known as FIPASS), situated to the east of The Narrows and about 3 km from the town centre, or at the Falkland Islands Company's East Jetty by prior arrangement with the company's shipping agency Fleetwing.

Permission to visit Crown Land, including small offshore islands, can be obtained from the Environmental Planning Office, Stanley. Some areas of land and offshore islands have been designated National Nature Reserves (Map 55). Within these areas, there are restrictions on camping and residence, and all plants and animals are protected. Entry into certain reserves may only be authorised by a visitor permit available from the Environmental Planning Office. Numerous privately owned islands are also managed as private reserves and permission must be obtained from the landowners prior to landing. Similarly, if you intend visiting farms or camp settlements, it is advisable to contact the farm owners or managers when planning your visit. The best source of information about who to contact, and other general enquiries, is the Falkland Islands Tourist Board and its visitor facility at the Jetty Centre, which has internet facilities and a wide selection of leaflets, brochures and books.

During the 1982 Anglo-Argentine conflict, many minefields were laid around Stanley and at several settlements out in camp.

All minefields are fenced off with clear warning signs placed along fencelines. However, these fences are not always visible from the sea, and for this reason it is vital that you obtain a copy of the minefield map from the Stanley Police Station in order to be able to locate the precise boundaries of minefields. If anchoring near a minefield, be aware that mines have been known to be washed from minefield shores onto adjacent beaches. If you think you have found an item of unexploded ordnance, do not touch it. Mark its position on the ground, make a note of its appearance, and then report it to the Stanley Police.

The British Forces operate several target practice and firing ranges on the islands. On some ranges, firing maybe directed to seaward of the range itself. The local radio broadcasts a daily 'ranges in use' summary and for more details contact the Stanley Police Station.

Wherever you go, take extreme care with fire: the peat soil burns *very* easily, particularly in the summer months: do not light a fire for any reason, and do not smoke in areas of tussac grass. If you see a fire, report it immediately to the Stanley Police Station.

The native plants and animals of the Falklands have been considerably modified by the introduction of large numbers of livestock (sheep, cattle, horses, reindeer, guanaco and goats), and by cats, rabbits, hares, Patagonian foxes, rats and mice.

Certain species of native plants, notably tussac grass, are now mostly confined to a few offshore islands. Native seabirds and seals are still abundant with vast numbers of black-browed albatross, and rockhopper, king, gentoo and Magellanic penguins, South American seal lions and fur seals. Minimise disturbance to wildlife by staying on the perimeter of breeding colonies, and avoid blocking seal and seabird routes to and from the sea. Remember that whalebones, eggs, skulls, etc. may not be exported from the Falkland Islands.

All native bird species are protected with the exception of upland geese, which may be killed all year round, and speckled and silver teal, which may be taken in the open season from 1 April to 30 June. The trout fishing season is from 1 September to 30 April, with a maximum take limit of six trout per day. Any fishing gear brought into the islands should be thoroughly cleaned before use in order to prevent accidental transmission of invasive freshwater algae and fish diseases. Hares, rabbits and Patagonian foxes are considered to be pests and may be hunted without a licence. However a firearms licence is necessary (available from the Stanley Police Station) and guns are not permitted to be fired within a three mile radius of Stanley. Permission to hunt and fish must be obtained beforehand from the landowner, with a fee sometimes charged by the landowner for access and river rights for fishing. Keep to paths wherever possible, and take care when crossing fences to pass between the wires rather than stepping on them, after checking that it is not an electric fence! If you open a gate, be sure to close it behind you, and take all your rubbish back with you.

*Visit enquiries*

Falkland Islands Tourism Board, Stanley, Falkland Islands FIQQ 1ZZ United Kingdom. Tel: +500 27019. Email: tourism@fidc.org.fk

The Jetty Centre. Tel: +500 22281.

Customs and Immigration Department, Stanley. Fax: +500 27342. Email: admin@customs.gov.fk

Environmental Planning Office, Stanley. Tel: +500 27390.

*Publications*

Falklands Conservation and Summers, D. (2006) *Visitor Guide to the Falkland Islands.* WildGuides, Maidenhead.

Southby-Tailyour S.E. (1985) *Falkland Islands Shores.* Conway Maritime Press, London.

Falkland Islands Government (2006) *Falkland Islands Ports and Harbours Information.* Falkland Islands Government, Stanley.

Penguin News (2007) *Falkland Islands Visitor Guide.* Falkland Islands Tourist Board, Stanley.

*Websites*

www.falklandsailing.com

www.tourism.org.fk

www.sartma.com

www.falklandislands.com

www.horizon.co.fk

www.penguin-news.com
www.mercopress.com
www.falklandsconservation.com
www.falklands.gov.fk
www.sulivanshipping.com

## South Georgia

South Georgia and its offshore islands (Map 56), including Shag Rocks and Clerke Rocks, lie 1350 km east-southeast of the Falkland Islands. The island is a United Kingdom Overseas Territory, administered by the Government of South Georgia and the South Sandwich Islands (GSGSSI). The Commissioner for the Territory resides in Stanley in the Falkland Islands and is represented at South Georgia by Government Officers stationed at King Edward Point. In addition, a Deputy Postmaster and approximately 12 British Antarctic Survey (BAS) personnel live on the island in the winter months with up to 20 additional personnel in summer.

Permission to visit is required from the Commissioner and applications should be made in writing by completing a visitor application form, available from the Commissioner or at the government website (www.sgisland.org). Visitors who plan to camp are required to complete an expedition application form, which is assessed by a panel of experts and attracts an administration fee of £1000.

Completed application forms should be returned to the Commissioner no later than 60 days before your intended visit. A permit is issued on the understanding that

you agree to abide by the guidelines and regulations contained in the document 'Information for Visitors to South Georgia' (available at www.sgisland.org). Post-Visit Report forms should be completed during your visit and returned to the Government Officer (King Edward Point) within 30 days of the end of your stay.

All vessels arriving at South Georgia should make contact with the Government Officer at King Edward Point as soon as practicable after entering the 200 nm Maritime Zone. Contact can be made by radio (call sign 'South Georgia Fisheries') on HF 4049 KHz USB between 1100–1200 GMT, or VHF Channel 16 (24 hours), or by email, fax, telex or satellite phone. Note that 2182 kHz is not monitored locally. The first place of landing for all vessels is King Edward Point where the Government Officer will carry out immigration, customs and port clearance formalities, brief visitors on current regulations and issue a complimentary Visitors Welcome Pack. Copies of the publication *Visitors Guide to South Georgia* are available at the Museum and Post Office. Harbour dues for yachts are currently £60. A landing fee of £100 is charged for each passenger on board, but no charge is made for crew members of any vessel, including yachts. With permission from the Government Officer, yachts may berth alongside the Tijuca jetty at Grytviken, or the King Edward Point jetty.

Conservation and protection of native species is regulated by the 1975 Falkland Islands Dependencies Conservation Or-

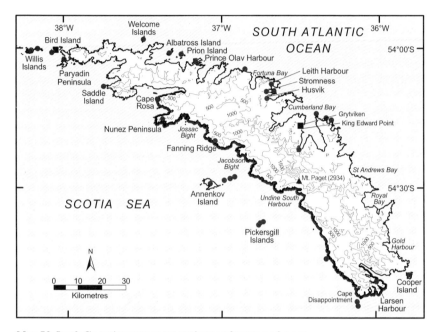

Map 56. South Georgia: permanent stations and protected areas

dinance and all native mammals, birds and plants are protected. Disturbance, killing, capture or export of native fauna and collection or destruction of native flora is prohibited, except by permit. No pet animals (e.g. cats, dogs) are permitted on the island. Strict rodent quarantine measures and bootwashing procedures apply in order to protect South Georgia from further introduction or translocation of alien species and disease. The Government Officer will provide biocide for boot washing and oversee biosecurity precautions. All visitors are required to sign a declaration confirming compliance with the required preventative measures issued by government.

Vessels carrying 12 persons or less may discharge sewage, food waste (excluding poultry waste) and grey water within 12 nautical miles of the shore, although preferably not in enclosed bays. Larger vessels are required to use sewage and waste macerator disposal units (mesh size <25mm) and to discharge outside the 12 nautical mile limit. All other wastes, including poultry waste, should be removed for disposal or recycling outside South Georgia. Open burning is prohibited but small campfires and smoking are allowed.

Shore-based expeditions should carry all waste and all equipment out and return it to the support vessel. Grey water should be drained into absorbent soil away from fresh water. Toilet waste should be disposed of directly in the sea or by burial in a shallow hole, well away from fresh water. There are several field huts around the island which are used intermittently by BAS, government personnel and expeditions. Do not use any equipment or food in these huts except in an emergency (in this event, notify a government representative of any supplies used so they may be restocked). Make sure all doors and windows are securely closed behind you when leaving.

Protected areas have been designated to provide a high level of protection to areas of special conservation or scientific interest, to areas which are rat-free, areas which are restricted due to health and safety concerns, and to heritage sites and sites designated for monitoring. Entry into protected areas is prohibited except with site-specific permission from the Government of South Georgia. Anchoring or cruising inshore and in bays close to protected areas is allowed. Designated protected areas include all whaling stations with the exception of Grytviken, and all rat-free areas, including Annenkov Island, Cooper Island, Willis Islands, Bird Island, Paryadin Peninsula, Nunez Peninsula, Albatross Island and Prion Island. Note that Bird Island is the site of a permanently occupied research station operated by the British Antarctic Survey and visitors require both a permit from government and permission from BAS.

*Visit enquiries*

The Commissioner of South Georgia and the South Sandwich Islands, Government House, Stanley, Falkland Islands FIQQ 1ZZ, United Kingdom. Tel: +500 27433, Fax: +500 27434. Email: gov.house@fco. gov.uk

The Government Officer, King Edward Point, South Georgia SIQQ 1ZZ, United Kingdom. Tel: (Inmarsat) +870 382 359 033. Fax: +870 382 359 034. Telex: 580 492 348 018 (Inmarsat C). Email: mo@ south-georgia.demon.co.uk

*Publications*

Carr, T. and Carr, P. (1998) *Antarctic Oasis*. W.W. Norton, London.

McIntosh, E. and Walton, D.W.H. (eds) (2000) *Environmental Management Plan for South Georgia*. On behalf of the Government of South Georgia and the South Sandwich Islands, British Antarctic Survey, Cambridge.

Burton, R. (1997). *South Georgia*. The Commissioner, Government of South Georgia and South Sandwich Islands.

Headland, R.K. (1984) *The Island of South Georgia*. Cambridge University Press, Cambridge.

Pasteur, E. and Walton, D.W.H. (eds) (2006) *South Georgia: Plan for Progress. Managing the Environment 2006-2010*. On behalf of the Government of South Georgia and the South Sandwich Islands, British Antarctic Survey, Cambridge.

Poncet, S. and Crosbie, K. (2005) *A Visitor's Guide to South Georgia*. WildGuides, Maidenhead.

Wheeler, T. (2004) *The Falklands and South Georgia Island.* Lonely Planet, Victoria, Australia.

*Websites*
Government of South Georgia:
www.sgisland.org
South Georgia Association:
www.southgeorgiaassociation.org
South Georgia Heritage Trust:
www.sght.org
South Georgia Surveys:
www.southgeorgiasurveys.org

*Essential documents*
Available on www.sgisland.org
• Expedition Guidelines
• Expedition Application Form
• South Georgia Prion Island Code of Conduct
• South Georgia Prion Island Post Visit Report Form
• South Georgia Post Visit Site Form
• South Georgia Information for Visitors Booklet (2006)
• South Georgia Biosecurity Self Audit Check list and Landing Declaration for all Visitors (2007)
• South Georgia Biosecurity Measures for all vessels landing passengers, crew, expedition staff or stores on South Georgia (2007).

**South Sandwich islands**
This group of 11 islands lies 530 km east-southeast of South Georgia. They are a United Kingdom Overseas Territory, administered by the Commissioner of the Government of South Georgia and the South Sandwich Islands (GSGSSI). The same regulations apply to visits here as at South Georgia. Under the 1975 Falkland Islands Dependencies Ordinance all native plants and animals are protected. No specially protected areas have been designated.

**Gough Island**
Lying 450 km southeast of Tristan da Cunha in the South Atlantic Ocean, Gough Island ($40°20'$S, $10°00'$W) is part of the British Overseas Territory of St Helena, and administered by the Administrator of Tristan da Cunha. Gough Island and neighbouring Inaccessible Island are designated as a strict Wildlife Reserve and are listed as a World Heritage Site. All native birds, mammals and plants are protected.

The South African Weather Bureau operates a permanent research and meteorological station at Transvaal Bay on the island's east coast. Tourism is not allowed and landings are prohibited unless prior written approval has been obtained from the Administrator.

*Visit enquiries*
The Administrator, Edinburgh, Tristan da Cunha, c/o The Foreign and Commonwealth Office, West Indian and Atlantic Department, London, SW1A 2AH, United Kingdom. Email: hmg@cunha.demon.co.uk

*Publications*
Cooper, J. and Ryan, P.G. (1994) Management Plan for the Gough Island Wildlife

Reserve. Government of Tristan da Cunha, Edinburgh, Tristan da Cunha.

**Bouvetøya**

Situated at 54°26'S, 03°24'E in the South Atlantic and 1600 km from the nearest land, Bouvetøya is the most isolated island in the world. The island and its adjacent territorial waters are a Norwegian possession and nature reserve, and the managing authority is the Norwegian Polar Institute. The entire island and its wildlife are protected and special permission is required to land. A summer research station and automatic weather station are located at Nyrøysa.

*Visit enquiries*

Norwegian Polar Institute, Polar Environmental Centre, N-9296 Tromsø, Norway (Norsk Polarinstitutt, Polarmiljøsenteret, 9296 Tromsø). Tel: + 47 77 75 05 00. Email: postmottak@npolar.no

*Websites*

Norwegian Polar Institute: http://npiweb.npolar.no

# South African sub-Antarctic islands

## Prince Edward Islands

The Prince Edward Islands (46°54'S, 37°45'E) consist of Marion Island (Map 57) and Prince Edward Island (Map 58). They are Special Nature Reserves, owned by South Africa and managed by the Department of Environmental Affairs and Tourism (DEA&T) in Pretoria.

All native wildlife and plants, and all sealers' and shipwreck remains are protected. Stringent precautions are taken to prevent accidental introductions of alien plants and animals, and tourism is not allowed.

**Marion Island** (46°54'S, 37°45'E) (Map 57) has a large and varied seabird breeding population, despite the presence of mice. A permanent meteorological station on the island's east coast at Transvaal Cove is run by the Weather Bureau for the DEA&T. The area around the station is classed as a Natural Zone where limited free walking is permitted. The remainder of the island is a Wilderness Zone and entry is by special permit for research only.

**Prince Edward Island** (46°38'S, 37°57'E) (Map 58) lying 22 km north-northeast of Marion Island, has been designated a Special Entry Area and is off-limits for all

**Map 57. Marion Island**

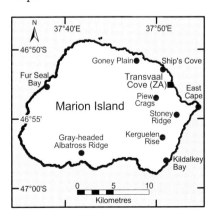

99

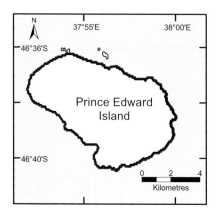

**Map 58. Prince Edward Island**

visitors, with the exception of scientists who are permitted one short visit each year under very strict permit conditions. The island is free of all introduced species and displays an exceptional abundance and diversity of seabirds.

*Visit enquiries*
The Director, Antarctica and Islands Division, Department of Environmental Affairs and Tourism, Private Bag X447, 0001 Pretoria, South Africa.

*Publications*
Prince Edward Islands Management Plan Working Group (1996) *The Prince Edward Islands Management Plan.* Department of Environmental Affairs and Tourism, Pretoria.
Chown, S. and Hänel, C. (1998) *An Introductory Guide to the Marion and Prince Edward Island Special Nature Reserves.* Department of Environmental Affairs and Tourism, Pretoria.

## French sub-Antarctic islands

The islands of Saint-Paul, Amsterdam, Crozet and Kerguelen are state-owned French Territory and form part of the Territoire des Terres Australes et Antarctiques Françaises (TAAF). These islands were declared a National Nature Reserve (la Reserve Naturelle de TAAF) under French legislation in October 2006, in order to protect marine mammals, plants and some bird species, and to regulate human activities. The reserve includes a large proportion of the territorial waters around Îles Kerguelen and Crozet (see Maps 61 and 63), within which all commercial activities, including fishing and hunting are prohibited, and only innocent passage of ships permitted. Landings are not permitted unless written authorisation has been obtained from the islands' Administrator in Île de la Réunion (TAAF, Saint Pierre), or from the Chefs de District at Îles Crozet, Kerguelen or Saint-Paul and Amsterdam. The French stations are the responsibility of TAAF and are administered from Île de la Réunion. Vessels are requested to ensure that their first port of call is at the TAAF station of each island group, and to contact the base commander upon arrival. A visitor's fee (15 Euros per day per person at the time of writing) and an anchorage fee (dependent on the size of vessel) are charged on arrival of the vessel and payable to the base commander.

**Île Amsterdam** (37°50'S, 77°35'E) (Map 59) lies 50 km north of Île Saint-Paul. A permanently manned TAAF research station, Martin-de-Viviés, is situated at La Cale on the northeast coast of Île Amsterdam, the first port of call for vessels visiting the archipelago.

Île Amsterdam has large populations of cattle, cats, rats and mice and there are very few remaining small seabirds. The entire island is a National Nature Reserve, with two sites of scientific interest protected in accordance with the TAAF Act of 1985: Plateau des Tourbières which occupies 20 sq km of the island's central plateau, and contains the only known colony (20 to 30 pairs) of the rare endemic Amsterdam albatross. The second is Entrecasteaux cliffs, a 1.5 km stretch of coastline from Fausse Pointe to Pointe d'Entrecasteaux on the west coast, where large numbers of yellow-nosed albatross and rockhopper penguins breed. Access to both sites is restricted in order to protect scientific research programmes.

Île Saint-Paul (38°43'S, 77°31'E) (Map 60), to the south of Île Amsterdam, is a National Nature Reserve. It is possible to anchor within the crater and the best landing is at the small jetty near the field hut that is regularly visited by TAAF personnel from Île Amsterdam. The island has been severely affected by man and introduced animals. Rats and rabbits were recently eradicated from the island and increasing numbers of small seabirds are breeding, moving in from nearby La Roche Quille. This rock

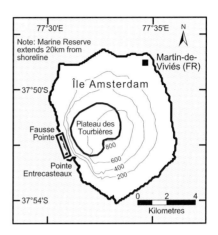

Map 59. Île Amsterdam

stack lies 150 m off Île Saint-Paul and is free of introduced animals, forming the last refuge for the bird species that previously existed in vast numbers in the archipelago. Because of its small area and the fact that some bird species are represented by only a few individuals, no landings are permitted on the stack.

Map 60. Île Saint-Paul

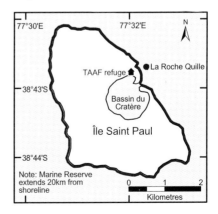

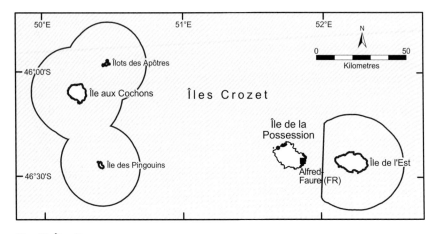

Map 61. Îles Crozet

Îles Crozet (46°26'S, 51°00'E) (Map 61), is an archipelago of five main islands (divided into a western and an eastern group), all of which are National Nature Reserves. With the exception of Île de la Possession, they are also protected areas under the 2007 TAAF decree. The islands host more breeding seabird species (36) than any other island group in the world. A permanent research station, Alfred-Faure, is situated on the east coast of Île de la Possession at Port Alfred, the first port of call for visiting vessels. The landing site is at the Baie du Marin, about 500 m from the base. Permission to visit should be obtained from the Administrator in Île de la Réunion, or from the Chef de District at Port Alfred.

The west group of islands is composed of Île des Pingouins, Îlots des Apôtres and Île aux Cochons. All are fully protected and no landings are permitted. The first two are the only localities in the archipelago that have never had introduced mammals, and are thus among the last places representative of the original flora and fauna of the region, with huge colonies of albatross, penguins and burrowing petrels. Despite the presence of introduced mice and cats, Île aux Cochons hosts 18 seabird species, and the world's largest king penguin colony.

The east group, consisting of Île de la Possession (Map 62) and Île de l'Est, lies 100 km SE of the western islands. Île de l'Est is free of cats and rats, and although rabbits have modified the original vegetation, there are still large numbers of burrowing petrels, and in all 30 species of breeding seabirds.

Île de la Possession (Map 62) is the largest island in the group, and despite the devastation to burrowing petrels caused by rats, the island retains some notable flora and fauna. There are several protected sites on the island where entry is only permitted for research purposes. They include a 10 km cliff coastline (with a 100 m buffer zone) between Crique de la Chaloupe and Crique de Noël which is a breeding site for light-mantled sooty albatross; gentoo penguin colonies in Baie du Marin, Criques du Sphinx, de la Chaloupe, de Noël, Baie Américaine; and the slopes close SW of the station Alfred-Faure where a colony of white-chinned petrels is located; Pointe Basse and Jardin Japonais which are long-term seabird monitoring sites.

**Îles Kerguelen** (48°00'S, 68°45'E) (Map 63) is an archipelago comprising one

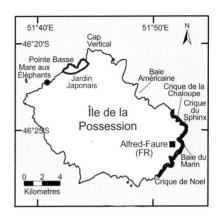

Map 62. Île de la Possession

large island (Grande Terre) and about 300 off-lying islands and rocks, all of which are National Nature Reserves. A permanently

Map 63. Îles Kerguelen

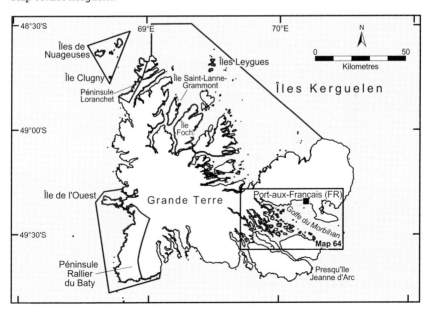

occupied TAAF research station, Port-aux-Français, accommodating up to 100 people in summer is situated in the Golfe du Morbihan on the east coast of Grande Terre. Permission to visit should be obtained from the Administrator in Réunion. Port-aux-Français is the first port of call for vessels.

Some areas have been designated protected areas under the 2007 decree. These are: the Péninsule Rallier du Baty, Îles Nuagueses, Îles Leygues, Île Clugny, Île de l'Ouest, Île Saint-Lanne-Grammont, Île Foch, islands in the **Golfe du Morbihan** (Map 64) (Hoskyn, Pender, Bryer, Blackeney, Greak, Suhm and Antarès). The introduction of numerous mammals has profoundly modified the native flora and fauna on most of Grande Terre, and these islands form the last

refuges for Kerguelen's remaining native populations. Some sites and islands are also of scientific interest, and entry is permitted only for research purposes. They include Île Foch, islands in the Golfe du Morbihan (Map 64), the west coast of Péninsule Rallier du Baty, Île Haute, Île du Cimetière, Île Australia, Île du Château, and the black-browed albatross colony at the east end of the Presqu'île Jeanne d'Arc.

*Visit enquiries*
Monsieur le Préfet, Administrateur Supérieur, Terres Australes et Antarctiques Françaises, rue Gabriel Dejean, BP 400, 97458 Saint-Pierre Cedex, Île de la Réunion.

Le Chef de District, Base Alfred-Faure, Crozet, Terres Australes et Antarctiques Françaises. Email: discro@cro-taaf.fr

**Map 64. Golfe du Morbihan, Îles Kerguelen**

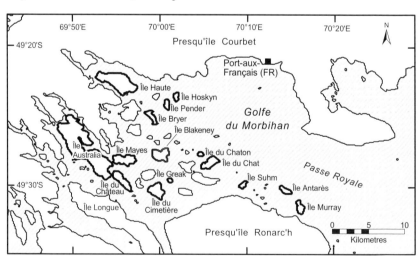

Le Chef de District, Base Port-aux-Français, Îles Kerguelen, Terres Australes et Antarctiques Françaises. Email: disker@ker-taaf.fr

Le Chef de District, Saint-Paul et Amsterdam, Terres Australes et Antarctiques Françaises. Email: disams @ams-taaf.fr

You can also contact the base commander by VHF radio (channels 6, 8, 9, 10, 12, 14, 16, 26, 27, 69, 71, 72, 73, 74, 77) and by HF radio on 3,885 Mhz.

*Websites*
Territoire des Terres Australes et
   Antarctiques Françaises:
   www.taaf.fr

## Australian sub-Antarctic islands

Australia has two sub-Antarctic outposts: the Heard Island and McDonald Islands group (Map 65), which are an Australian external Territory, and Macquarie Island (Map 66), which is part of the Australian state of Tasmania.

The Territory of Heard Island and McDonald Islands comprises the islands and the 12 nautical mile territorial sea (Map 65). It was listed as a World Heritage Area in 1997 for its outstanding natural universal values. It is the only major sub-Antarctic island group believed to contain no species directly introduced by humans, and one of the most biologically pristine locations in the world. The Heard Island and McDonald Islands Marine Reserve (65,000 km$^2$) was declared in 2002 and includes the Territory plus additional marine areas that extend in parts to the 200 nm Exclusive Economic Zone boundary. The Territory and Marine Reserve are managed by the Australian Antarctic Division of the Department of the Environment and Water Resources, in accordance with the Heard Island and McDonald Islands Marine Reserve Management Plan 2005, the Environment Protection and Biodiversity Conservation Act 1999, the Environment Protection and Management Ordinance 1987 (EPMO) and other relevant legislation.

A permit from the Australian Antarctic Division is required to enter the Territory other than on innocent passage. It is important to note that for quarantine reasons, visits to Heard Island by vessels travelling from other sub-Antarctic locations may not be permitted. The management plan for the Marine Reserve details visitor access zones, strict quarantine requirements, an environmental impact assessment process for proposed activities and other measures to provide for the comprehensive protection of the environment and wildlife of the islands and surrounding waters. It is an offence to import live organisms or dead poultry; to injure, interfere with or remove any indigenous organism; to leave any equipment, material or refuse ashore; to collect any material – alive or dead; to interfere with any buildings, relics, supplies, scientific experiments or survey markers.

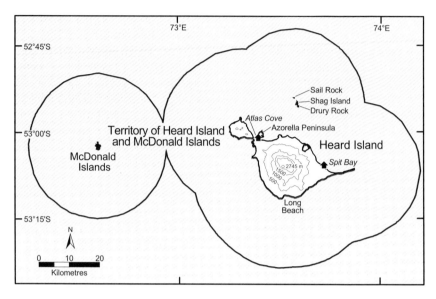

Map 65. Heard Island and McDonald Islands

Heard Island (53°05'S, 73°30'E) (Map 65) has no introduced mammals and only one non-native plant species (believed to have arrived by natural means). The island provides crucial breeding habitat for a range of birds and marine mammals, including several threatened and migratory species protected under legislation and international agreements. No permanent facilities are located on the island, although there are several temporary refuges located at Atlas Cove and Spit Bay. The heritage-listed remains of a research station, occupied from 1947 to 1954 by the Australian National Antarctic Research Expedition (ANARE), are found at Atlas Cove on Laurens Peninsula. Scientific expeditions undertaken every few years are the main human activity on the island.

McDonald Islands (53°03'S, 72°36'E) (Map 65), lying 40 km west of Heard Island, are volcanically active, with the main island almost doubling in size between 1980 and 2004. The islands are completely closed to tourism and other activities excepting those undertaken for approved research or management purposes.

*Visit enquiries*
Environmental Policy and Protection Section, Australian Antarctic Division, Channel Highway, Kingston, Tasmania, 7050, Australia. Email: himi@aad.gov.au

*Publications*
Australian Antarctic Division (2005). *Heard Island and McDonald Islands Marine Reserve Management Plan.*

Australian Antarctic Division of the Department of the Environment and Water Resources, Hobart. Download from www.heardisland.aq

*Websites*
www.heardisland.aq
www.aad.gov.au

**Macquarie Island** (54°30'S, 158°55'E) (Map 66) and the nearby islands of Judge and Clerk, and Bishop and Clerk lie approximately 1500 km south of New Zealand and Tasmania. The islands are part of the State of Tasmania and are administered as a Nature Reserve under Tasmania's National Parks and Reserves Management Act 2002. Macquarie Island is also designated a World Heritage Area and an International Biosphere Reserve. The Macquarie Island Marine Park extends out to 200 nm on the eastern side of the reserve, encompassing an area of 162,000 km$^2$. The islands and surrounding waters out to 3 nm are a restricted area and all persons wanting to visit must obtain an access authority from the Tasmanian Parks and Wildlife Service.

No access is permitted to Judge and Clerk, or Bishop and Clerk. All visits to Macquarie Island are subject to strict environmental and quarantine controls designed to minimise environmental impact and to protect the island's wildlife and other natural and cultural values. Landings are only allowed at two locations (The Isthmus and Sandy Bay) and all visits are supervised by Parks and Wildlife Service

staff. Visits ashore are permitted between 0700 and 1900 local station time with no overnight stays ashore allowed. The scientific station at the northern tip of the island is permanently staffed by scientific and support personnel from the Australian Antarctic Division and visits to the station are at the discretion of the Station Leader. A landing fee of AUS $165 is made for each person onboard a private vessel.

*Visit enquiries*
Tasmanian Parks and Wildlife Service, GPO Box 1751, Hobart 7001, Tasmania, Australia. Email: himi@aad.gov.au

**Map 66. Macquarie Island**

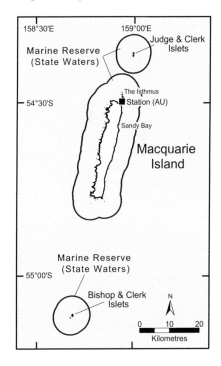

107

*Publications*
*Guidelines for Tourist Operations and Visits to Macquarie Island.* Download from www.parks.tas.gov.au/macquarie/guidelines.html
Tasmanian Parks and Wildlife Service (2001) Macquarie Island, *Visitors Guidebook.* Tasmanian Parks and Wildlife Service, Hobart, Tasmania.
Parks and Wildlife Service (2006) *Macquarie Island Nature Reserve and World Heritage Area.*
*Management Plan*, Parks and Wildlife Service, Department of Tourism, Arts and the Environment, Hobart. Download from:www.parks.tas.gov.au/publications/tech/macquarie/summary.html

*Websites*
www.parks.tas.gov.au/macquarie/index.html
www.aad.gov.au

# New Zealand's sub-Antarctic islands

New Zealand's sub-Antarctic islands include Campbell, Auckland, Antipodes, Bounty and Snares (Map 1). They lie to the south and east of New Zealand and are New Zealand territory administered by the Department of Conservation (DOC) Southern Islands Area Manager. While research parties are often in residence, none of the islands have a permanent human population and they are managed as National Nature Reserves, with regular surveillance by New Zealand aircraft and ships. They are designated as a World Heritage Area. The indigenous flora and fauna are protected by the Reserves Act 1977 and other New Zealand statutes, and all marine mammals are protected under the Marine Mammals Protection Act 1978. A minimum impact code applies to all visitors, in order to minimise disturbance to wildlife, plants and other natural features.

All visits to these islands are subject to strict quarantine procedures to ensure that there are no accidental introductions of alien species, particularly rats, but also invertebrates, plants (seeds) and micro-organisms. Quarantine inspection is carried out by DOC at Bluff, the main port of departure for cruise ships visiting the islands. No pets (or any other animals) are permitted on board.

DOC's guidelines for tourism are stringent. Landing and entry to the islands is by permit only upon application to DOC. The permit will state where you can land and how many people, which ensures that the quotas are not exceeded. A landing fee of NZ$250 is charged per person, with a minimum charge of NZ$2500 for commercial operations. Activities other than tourism, e.g. mountaineering, filming, and the collection of specimens, must be covered by a separate agreement and permit. Landings for a total of 600 people per season (i.e. July to June) are permitted at the site of the former base in Perseverance Harbour on Campbell Island, and at Enderby Island and the Hardwicke settlement site at the Auckland

Islands, and 150 people at the other approved open sites. Note that landings are only permitted on main Campbell, main Auckland and Enderby islands. All other sites and islands are strictly out of bounds. All visitors, whether passengers on board cruise ships (150 passengers maximum), small tour boats (50 people maximum) or yachts (2-9 people, non-profit-seeking) are to be accompanied by a departmental representative accredited by DOC. In the case of all commercial operations this must be a departmental staff member (or guide), with a maximum ratio of 20 visitors: 1 guide.

All tourist operations are ship-based with no overnight stays on the islands allowed. The day's programme must be approved by the DOC representative (guide) before landing. No collecting of specimens or souvenirs is permitted. Keep a minimum of 5 metres from all wildlife, and increase this if there is any sign of disturbance or if you are on an animal or bird access way. All shore parties are to be in 2-way radio communication with the ship, and have emergency equipment and first aid kits. Sufficient experienced personnel must be left on board the vessel to be able to operate it at all times in case of an emergency. Food and drink items consumed on shore are to be pre-packed, unopened and approved by the DOC. Smoking is not allowed while ashore, except on the shoreline at least 5 m away from any vegetation, since the peat soils and dry vegetation during summer can create conditions of high fire risk. There

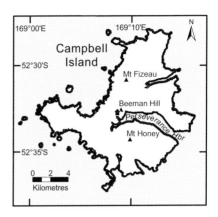

**Map 67. Campbell Island**

are no facilities (e.g. toilets) provided for tourists onshore.

All bags, pockets, footwear etc. must be inspected for soil and seeds and cleaned before each landing; footwear must be cleaned using a biocide between landings.

**Campbell Island** (52°33'S, 169°09'E) (Map 67) is open to visitors with permits. Landings for up to 150 people at any one time on any day are permitted at the wharf at the former base in Perseverance Harbour, from where visitors can access a boardwalk up to the Col-Lyall Saddle. Only 50 people a day are permitted to land at the other approved sites on any day. The DOC guide may permit landings of small parties elsewhere specifically to reduce the impact of overland travel. No access is permitted in the area north of Mt. Fizeau to Mt. Azimuth or onto Beeman Hill.

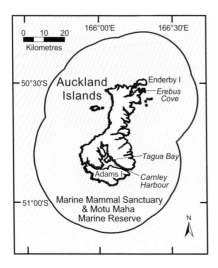

**Map 68. Auckland Islands**

**Auckland Islands** (50° 50'S, 166° 00'E) (Map 68) and including Enderby Island. All inshore waters out to 12 nautical miles around these islands are a Marine Reserve and marine mammal sanctuary where fishing, the taking of any marine life and the disposal of ALL wastes, including of grey water, are prohibited.

**Enderby Island** (Map 68) is open to visitors under permit (150 maximum ashore at any one time on any day). The landing site is on the beach at Sandy Bay. In December and January during the Hooker's sea lions' breeding season, visitors must cross the beach using a single entry and exit site determined by the guide, and they must avoid the main access ways for the yellow-eyed penguin. Restrictions on party size and movements at Enderby Island may be enforced by

the party guide according to the timing of the breeding season of the Hooker's sea lions.

Hardwicke in Erebus Cove on Auckland Island is also open to visitors under permit (150 maximum ashore at any one time on any day). A maximum of 50 people per day can land at the other approved sites on the main island. No cruise ship is to proceed up Carnley Harbour beyond Tagua Bay.

**Antipodes Islands** (49°41'S, 178°48'E) **and Bounty Islands**, (47°42'S 179°03'E) are not open to tourism. Landings are not permitted, but Zodiac cruising within the groups is possible.

**Snares Islands** (48°02'S, 166°35'E) are visited by small groups of researchers who use the small field hut on the island's east coast but tourist landings are prohibited. Zodiac cruising is permitted. Anchoring at these islands is not encouraged, and use of mooring lines is prohibited, with the exception of a single licensed fishing vessel with a mooring permit for Hoho Bay. Strict quarantine measures are imposed by both the government and the fishermen themselves to minimise the risk of rodent introduction.

*Visit enquiries*
Southland Area Manager, Department of Conservation (DOC) Southland Conservancy, PO Box 743, Invercargill, New Zealand. Tel: +64 3 2144589. Email: invercargill@doc.govt.nz

*Publications*

Peat, N. (2006) *Subantarctic New Zealand – a rare heritage.* Department of Conservation Te Papa Atawhai, Wellington.

*Websites*

Department of Conservation: www.doc.govt.nz/templates/PlaceProfile. aspx?id=35670

# Annex I: Guidance for Visitors to the Antarctic

Activities in the Antarctic are governed by the Antarctic Treaty of 1959 and associated agreements, referred to collectively as the Antarctic Treaty system. The Treaty established Antarctica as a zone of peace and science.

In 1991, the Antarctic Treaty Consultative Parties adopted the Protocol on Environmental Protection to the Antarctic Treaty, which designates the Antarctic as a natural reserve. The Protocol sets out environmental principles, procedures and obligations for the comprehensive protection of the Antarctic environment, and its dependent and associated ecosystems. The Consultative Parties have agreed that, pending its entry into force, as far as possible and in accordance with their legal system, the provisions of the Protocol should be applied as appropriate.

The Environmental Protocol applies to tourism and non-governmental activities as well as governmental activities in the Antarctic Treaty area. It is intended to ensure that these activities do not have adverse impacts on the Antarctic environment, or on its scientific and aesthetic values.

This Guidance for Visitors to the Antarctic is intended to ensure that all visitors are aware of, and are therefore able to comply with, the Treaty and the Protocol. Visitors are, of course, bound by national laws and regulations applicable to activities in the Antarctic.

## A) Protect Antarctic wildlife

Taking or harmful interference with Antarctic wildlife is prohibited except in accordance with a permit issued by a national authority.

1. Do not use aircraft, vessels, small boats, or other means of transport in ways that disturb wildlife, either at sea or on land.
2. Do not feed, touch, or handle birds or seals, or approach or photograph them in ways that cause them to alter their behavior. Special care is needed when animals are breeding or moulting.
3. Do not damage plants, for example by walking, driving, or landing on extensive moss beds or lichen-covered scree slopes.
4. Do not use guns or explosives. Keep noise to the minimum to avoid frightening wildlife.
5. Do not bring non-native plants or animals into the Antarctic (e.g. live poultry, pet dogs and cats, house plants).

## B) Respect protected areas

A variety of areas in the Antarctic have been afforded special protection because of their particular ecological, scientific, historic or other values. Entry into certain areas may be prohibited except in accordance with a permit issued by an appropriate national authority. Activities in and near designated Historic Sites and Monuments and certain other areas may be subject to special restrictions.

1. Know the locations of areas that have been afforded special protection and any restrictions regarding entry and activities that can be carried out in and near them.
2. Observe applicable restrictions.
3. Do not damage, remove or destroy Historic Sites or Monuments, or any artefacts associated with them.

### C) Respect scientific research

Do not interfere with scientific research, facilities or equipment.

1. Obtain permission before visiting Antarctic science and logistic support facilities; reconfirm arrangements 24-72 hours before arriving; and comply strictly with the rules regarding such visits.
2. Do not interfere with, or remove, scientific equipment or marker posts, and do not disturb experimental study sites, field camps or supplies.

### D) Be safe

Be prepared for severe and changeable weather. Ensure that your equipment and clothing meet Antarctic standards. Remember that the Antarctic environment is inhospitable, unpredictable and potentially dangerous.

1. Know your capabilities, the dangers posed by the Antarctic environment, and act accordingly. Plan activities with safety in mind at all times.
2. Keep a safe distance from all wildlife, both on land and at sea.
3. Take note of, and act on, the advice and instructions from your leaders; do not stray from your group.

4. Do not walk onto glaciers or large snow fields without proper equipment and experience; there is a real danger of falling into hidden crevasses.
5. Do not expect a rescue service; self-sufficiency is increased and risks reduced by sound planning, quality equipment, and trained personnel.
6. Do not enter emergency refuges (except in emergencies). If you use equipment or food from a refuge, inform the nearest research station or national authority once the emergency is over.
7. Respect any smoking restrictions, particularly around buildings, and take great care to safeguard against the danger of fire. This is a real hazard in the dry environment of Antarctica.

### E) Keep Antarctica pristine

Antarctica remains relatively pristine, and has not yet been subjected to large scale human perturbations. It is the largest wilderness area on earth. Please keep it that way.

1. Do not dispose of litter or garbage on land. Open burning is prohibited.
2. Do not disturb or pollute lakes or streams. Any materials discarded at sea must be disposed of properly.
3. Do not paint or engrave names or graffiti on rocks or buildings.
4. Do not collect or take away biological or geological specimens or man-made artefacts as a souvenir, including rocks, bones, eggs, fossils, and parts or contents of buildings.
5. Do not deface or vandalise buildings, whether occupied, abandoned, or un-occupied, or emergency refuges.

## Annex II: Guidance for those Organising and Conducting Tourism and Non-governmental Activities in the Antarctic

Antarctica is the largest wilderness area on earth, unaffected by large scale human activities. Accordingly, this unique and pristine environment has been afforded special protection. Furthermore, it is physically remote, inhospitable, unpredictable and potentially dangerous. All activities in the Antarctic Treaty area, therefore, should be planned and conducted with both environmental protection and safety in mind.

Activities in the Antarctic are subject to the Antarctic Treaty of 1959 and associated legal instruments, referred to collectively as the Antarctic Treaty system. These include the Convention for the Conservation of Antarctic Seals (CCAS' 1972), the Convention on the Conservation of Antarctic Marine Living Resources (CCAMLR' 1980) and the Recommendations and other measures adopted by the Antarctic Treaty Consultative Parties under the Antarctic Treaty.

In 1991, the Consultative Parties to the Antarctic Treaty adopted the Protocol on Environmental Protection to the Antarctic Treaty. This Protocol sets out environmental principles, procedures and obligations for the comprehensive protection of the Antarctic environment, and its dependent and associated ecosystems. The Consultative Parties have agreed that, pending its entry into force, as far as possible and in accordance with their legal systems, that the

provisions of the Protocol should be applied as appropriate.

The Environmental Protocol designates Antarctica as a natural reserve devoted to peace and science, and applies to both governmental and non-governmental activities in the Antarctic Treaty area. The Protocol seeks to ensure that human activities, including tourism, do not have adverse impacts on the Antarctic environment, nor on its scientific and aesthetic values.

The Protocol states, as a matter of principle, that all activities are to be planned and conducted on the basis of information sufficient to evaluate their possible impact on the Antarctic environment and its associated ecosystems, and on the value of Antarctica for the conduct of scientific research. Organisers should be aware that the Environmental Protocol requires that "activities shall be modified, suspended or cancelled if they result in or threaten to result in impacts upon the Antarctic environment or dependent or associated ecosystems."

Those responsible for organising and conducting tourism and non governmental activities must comply fully with national laws and regulations which implement the Antarctic Treaty system, as well as other national laws and regulations implementing international agreements on environmental

ANNEX II: GUIDANCE FOR TOUR OPERATORS AND NGOS

protection, pollution and safety that relate to the Antarctic Treaty area. They should also abide by the requirements imposed on organisers and operators under the Protocol on Environmental Protection and its Annexes, in so far as they have not yet been implemented in national law.

**Key obligations on organisers and operators**

1. Provide prior notification of, and reports on, their activities to the competent authorities of the appropriate Party or Parties.
2. Conduct an assessment of the potential environmental impacts of their planned activities.
3. Provide for effective response to environmental emergencies, especially with regard to marine pollution.
4. Ensure self-sufficiency and safe operations.
5. Respect scientific research and the Antarctic environment, including restrictions regarding protected areas, and the protection of flora and fauna.
6. Prevent the disposal and discharge of prohibited waste.

**Procedures to be followed by organisers and operators**

*A. When planning to go to the Antarctic - organisers and operators should:*

1. Notify the competent national authorities of the appropriate Party or Parties of details of their planned activities with sufficient time to enable the Party(ies) to comply with their information exchange obligations under Article VII(5) of the

Antarctic Treaty. The information to be provided is listed in Attachment A.
2. Conduct an environmental assessment in accordance with such procedures as may have been established in national law to give effect to Annex I of the Protocol, including, if appropriate, how potential impacts will be monitored.
3. Obtain timely permission from the national authorities responsible for any stations they propose to visit.
4. Provide information to assist in the preparation of: contingency response plans in accordance with Article 15 of the Protocol; waste management plans in accordance with Annex III of the Protocol; and marine pollution contingency plans in accordance with Annex IV of the Protocol.
5. Ensure that expedition leaders and passengers are aware of the location and special regimes which apply to Specially Protected Areas and Sites of Special Scientific Interest (and on entry into force of the Protocol, Antarctic Specially Protected Areas and Antarctic Specially Managed Areas) and of Historic Sites and Monuments and, in particular, relevant management plans.
6. Obtain a permit, where required by national law, from the competent national authority of the appropriate Party or Parties, should they have a reason to enter such areas, or a monitoring site (CEMP Site) designated under CCAMLR.
7. Ensure that activities are fully self-sufficient and do not require assistance from Parties unless arrangements for it have been agreed in advance.
8. Ensure that they employ experienced and

115

trained personnel, including a sufficient number of guides.

9. Arrange to use equipment, vehicles, vessels, and aircraft appropriate to Antarctic operations.

10. Be fully conversant with applicable communications, navigation, air traffic control and emergency procedures.

11. Obtain the best available maps and hydrographic charts, recognising that many areas are not fully or accurately surveyed.

12. Consider the question of insurance (subject to requirements of national law).

13. Design and conduct information and education programmes to ensure that all personnel and visitors are aware of relevant provisions of the Antarctic Treaty system.

14. Provide visitors with a copy of the Guidance for Visitors to the Antarctic.

*B. When in the Antarctic Treaty area - organisers and operators should:*

1. Comply with all requirements of the Antarctic Treaty system,and relevant national laws, and ensure that visitors are aware of requirements that are relevant to them.

2. Reconfirm arrangements to visit stations 24-72 hours before their arrival and ensure that visitors are aware of any conditions or restrictions established by the station.

3. Ensure that visitors are supervised by a sufficient number of guides who have adequate experience and training in Antarctic conditions and knowledge of the Antarctic Treaty system requirements.

4. Monitor environmental impacts of their activities, if appropriate, and advise the competent national authorities of the appropriate Party or Parties of any adverse or cumulative impacts resulting from an activity, but which were not foreseen by their environmental impact assessment.

5. Operate ships, yachts, small boats, aircraft, hovercraft, and all other means of transport safely and according to appropriate procedures, including those set out in the Antarctic Flight Information Manual (AFIM).

6. Dispose of waste materials in accordance with Annex III and IV of the Protocol. These annexes prohibit, among other things, the discharge of plastics, oil and noxious substances into the Antarctic Treaty area; regulate the discharge of sewage and food waste; and require the removal of most wastes from the area.

7. Co-operate fully with observers designated by Consultative Parties to conduct inspections of stations, ships, aircraft and equipment under Article VII of the Antarctic Treaty, and those to be designated under Article 14 of the Environmental Protocol.

8. Co-operate in monitoring programmes undertaken in accordance with Article 3(2)(d) of the Protocol.

9. Maintain a careful and complete record of their activities conducted.

*C. On completion of the activities*
Within three months of the end of the activity, organisers and operators should report on

the conduct of it to the appropriate national authority in accordance with national laws and procedures. Reports should include the name, details and state of registration of each vessel or aircraft used and the name of their captain or commander; actual itinerary; the number of visitors engaged in the activity; places, dates and purposes of landings and the number of visitors landed on each occasion; any meteorological observations made, including those made as part of the World Meteorological Organization (WMO) Voluntary Observing Ships Scheme; any significant changes in activities and their impacts from those predicted before the visit was conducted; and action taken in case of emergency.

*D. Antarctic Treaty System documents and information*

Most Antarctic Treaty Parties can provide, through their national contact points, copies of relevant provisions of the Antarctic Treaty system and information about national laws and procedures, including:

- The Antarctic Treaty (1959)
- Convention on the Conservation of Antarctic Marine Living Resources (1980)
- Protocol on Environmental Protection to the Antarctic Treaty (1991)
- Recommendations and other measures adopted under the Antarctic Treaty
- Final Reports of Consultative Meetings
- Handbook of the Antarctic Treaty System (1994)
- Handbook of the Antarctic Treaty System (in Spanish, 1991).

**Attachment A**

*Information to be Provided in Advance Notice*

Organisers should provide the following information to the appropriate national authorities in the format requested.

1. Name, nationality, and contact details of the organiser;
2. Where relevant, registered name and national registration and type of any vessel or aircraft to be used (including name of the captain or commander, call-sign, radio frequency, INMARSAT number);
3. Intended itinerary including the date of departure and places to be visited in the Antarctic Treaty area;
4. Activities to be undertaken and purpose;
5. Number and qualifications of crew and accompanying guides and expedition staff;
6. Estimated number of visitors to be carried;
7. Carrying capacity of vessel;
8. Intended use of vessel;
9. Intended use and type of aircraft;
10. Number and type of other vessels, including small boats, to be used in the Antarctic Treaty area;
11. Information about insurance coverage;
12. Details of equipment to be used, including for safety purposes, and arrangements for self-sufficiency;
13. And other matters required by national laws.

# Annex III: Marine Wildlife Watching Guidelines
## International Association of Antarctica Tour Operators (IAATO)

The aim of these guidelines is to protect cetaceans, seals and seabirds by avoiding any harmful disturbance to normal behaviours, while ensuring a high quality wildlife-watching experience through responsible observation.

*Competent, careful boat handling and visitor management avoids harming wildlife and leads to better wildlife watching.*

## General principles for viewing wildlife

The animal/s should dictate all encounters: they will choose whether to stay with the vessel or move away. Respect their decision and *never* chase or pursue animals.

Experienced ship's officers and naturalists are often able to evaluate animal/s behaviour and can best judge if it is possible to carefully approach the animal/s or not.

In line with Recommendation XVIII-1 and IAATO general codes of conduct never attempt to touch or feed birds or animals.

### Whales, dolphins, porpoises & seals
When in an area known for marine mammals, vessel operators should keep a good lookout forward and always take care to avoid collisions: this may include stopping, slowing down, and / or steering away from the animal/s.

*Awareness of the animal/s' behavioural patterns:*
Animals may alter their behaviour if they are disturbed by your activities. If the cetacean is agitated or no longer interested in staying near the vessel, behavioural changes may be observed. When in doubt give animals their time and space.

*General code of conduct around marine mammals*
• Do not stay with the animal/s too long, with a suggested maximum time of 1 hour. If signs of disturbance occur retreat slowly and quietly.
• Never herd (circle), separate, scatter, or pursue a group of marine mammals, particularly mothers and young.
• If a cetacean approaches a vessel to bow-ride, maintain a relatively constant course and speed. Do not enter a group of dolphins to encourage them to bow-ride.
• Do not play back underwater sounds. This includes recorded whale or dolphin sounds.
• During any close encounters follow the guidelines below.

*Approaching cetaceans*
There should be no intentional approach within:
- 30 metres or 100 feet for small boats (including kayaks);

- 100 metres or 300 feet for small boats (including kayaks)[1] if cetaceans communally feeding;
- 100 metres or 300 feet for ships;
- 150m / 500 ft. if ship over 20,000 tons;
- 200m / 600 ft. if 2 ships present.

Helicopters or any aircraft should not approach closer than 300 metres or 1000 feet vertical distance. *Aircraft should cease contact if the animals repeatedly dive or increase speed.*

*Approaching from a distance*
Approximately 1500 to 3000 metres / one to two miles away:
• Reduce speed to 10 knots or less.
• Post a dedicated lookout to assist the vessel operator in monitoring the location of all marine mammals.
1500 to 750 metres / one to one-half mile away:
• Reduce speed to 5 knots.
Approximately 750 metres / half a mile or closer:
• Reduce speed to less than 5 knots.
• Manoeuvre vessel to avoid a head-on approach.
• Avoid sudden gear changes (e.g. into reverse).

*When in the final stage of approach*
Approximately 200 metres / 600 feet or closer:
• Approach at no faster than 'no-wake' speed or at idle, whichever is slower.

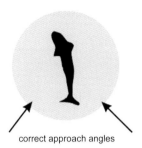

correct approach angles

• Approach the animal/s from parallel to and slightly to the rear (see figure above).
• Once travelling with the animal, travel parallel with it/them
• Stay clear of feeding baleen whales.
• Try to position the vessel downwind of the animals.
• Ensure good communication and co-ordination between vessels, small boats or Zodiacs in multi-vessel approaches.
• It is suggested not to have more than a maximum of two ships or four small craft watching each animal/s at a time.
• Ensure approaches are closely co-ordinated to avoid 'boxing-in' cetaceans, creating a 'tunnel' of small boats or kayaks, or crossing of their travel routes.
• Be aware of local geography – never 'trap' animals between the vessel and shore.
• Avoid sudden or repeated changes in direction, speed or changing gears when close to marine mammals.

*When in the optimal viewing area*
(Note: Ideally this should be no more than one vessel at a time.)

1. For the purposes of this information small boat is defined as a Zodiac, RIB, Naiad, Avon, Polarcirkle or similar small landing craft.

Approximately 30 metres / 100 feet for Zodiacs / 100 metres / 300 feet for ships:
- Should a vessel approach closer than the recommended minimum distance, withdraw at a constant, slow, no-wake speed, to at least the recommended minimum distance.
- When stopping to watch cetaceans, allow the motor to idle for several minutes before considering turning off.
- Avoid excess engine use, gear changes, maneuvering or backing up to the animals.
- Ships should avoid the use of bow or stern lateral thrusters to maintain position.
- Be aware that whales may surface in unexpected locations.
- Breaching, tail-lobbing or flipper slapping whales may be socialising and may not be aware of boats. Keep your distance.
- Feeding humpback whales often emit sub-surface bubbles before rising to feed at the surface. Avoid these light green bubble patches.
- Emitting periodic noise may help to let whales know your location and avoid whale and boat collisions.
- On some occasions animals may approach a vessel: in that instance put engines in neutral and do not re-engage propulsion until they are observed well clear of your vessel.
- Stay quiet and minimise passenger movement in small boats or Zodiacs during close encounters.
- Enjoy the experience.
(Note: Allowing a vessel to drift within accepted recommended distances could constitute an intentional approach.)

*When leaving the optimal viewing area*
- Move off at a slow 'no-wake' speed to the minimum distance of the optimal viewing area. Avoid engaging propellers within the minimum approach distance, if possible.
- Always move away from the animals to their rear, i.e., not in front of them.

**Hauled-out seals**
Seals hauled out on land, rock or ice can be sensitive to boats and human presence. Noises, smells and sights may elicit a reaction. Be aware of behaviours that indicate a seal has been disturbed. Such behaviours include, but are not limited to:
- An increase in alertness or vigilance, including head turning;
- Change in posture from lying to erect;
- Hurriedly moving away from the approaching vessel;
- Open mouth threat displays (similar to yawning);
- Aggressive displays or bluff charges in your direction.

*In essence, any seal response other than a raised head should be avoided.*

*General guidelines for viewing hauled-out seals*
- Hauled out seals should not be approached closer than 5 - 10 metres (15 - 30 feet).
- When viewing seals do not surround or separate them, especially mothers and pups. Stay to one side where they can see you.
- On beaches, avoid getting between seals and the sea; walk 'above' them, trying not

to break their horizon, or tower over them – stay low and quiet.

- Pups are often left alone when the mother is feeding. They are not abandoned and should be left alone and not touched.

- Keep commentary, conversation and engine noise to a minimum and be aware of your radio volume.

- If an individual or a herd moves towards the water or there is a hurried entry into the water by many individuals, you should retreat slowly and carefully.

- Be aware that fur seals and sea lions are highly mobile on land and might charge (and potentially bite) you if approached too closely.

- Be alert to animals hidden in tussock grass areas. Ideally, staff member should lead any tussock walks, carrying a walking stick or equivalent.

### Watching seabirds

*Vessel and small boat operations near birds*
Sometimes spectacular concentrations of seabirds may be found out at sea – rafts of birds either feeding on the surface, diving, or simply resting and bathing. Many of these birds may have flown hundreds or thousands of miles, often to find food for their young.

- Be aware of birds in the water, slow down and / or alter course to avoid collision.

- Stay on the fringes of these concentrations. Ships should stay 100 metres (300 feet) and small boats or Zodiacs 30 metres (100 feet) away.

- Birds such as penguins may be subject to disturbance by Zodiac operations close to landing sites or colonies.

- Approach or depart a landing site or colony slowly to minimise any disturbance.

- Avoid boat operations in waters close to where birds enter and exit, are bathing, or are feeding close to colonies.

- Staff/crew should assess the best landing point – ideally as far from the birds as possible. This is particularly important if birds are moulting near the shore.

- There may be occasions when swimming penguins find themselves in a Zodiac when they 'porpoise'. Occupants should remain quiet and wait for the penguin to find its own way out. It is normally not necessary to assist.

- Under no circumstances should 'chumming' (depositing fish guts or oil) or feeding of birds occur.

*Viewing birds ashore*
If parent birds are blocked from returning to their nests, increased predation of eggs and chicks by skuas and gulls may occur. In addition, parent birds will waste precious energy by avoiding human obstacles on their way to their nests.

- Walk slowly and encourage visitors to simply sit quietly and watch the animals.

- Avoid blocking 'walkways' in colonies, and water entry and exit points.

- Take care in tussock grass where birds may be nesting in burrows and walkways may be hidden by foliage.

- If skuas (jaegers) or terns start dive-bombing, they are protecting young or nests. Retreat in the direction you approached. Be aware that eggs and young are well camouflaged.

*Recommended approach distances*
- In general, keep 5-10 metres (15 – 30 feet) from nesting seabirds.
- Keep 10 metres (30 feet) from nesting, and 25 metres (75 feet) from displaying albatross on South Georgia.
- When on the same level as, or walking above, nesting giant petrels stay 25-50 metres (75 – 150 feet) away, if possible.

**Entanglement and strandings**
- Any animals entangled in fishing equipment etc., should be assisted where possible. Only use experienced staff/crew and take precautions – seal bites are particularly prone to disease.
- Photographs of the entanglement should be taken and a report sent to IAATO.
- Should you not be able to assist, please record details including geographic position (in latitude/longitude), species, and type of entanglement. Please report the event as soon as possible, so assistance may be sought from others.
- Details of dead (floating) animals and 'strandings' (beached) cetaceans should be recorded and reported to IAATO. If possible include photographs of the front and side of the head of the animal (for species identification) with a scale of measurement (e.g., a ruler or Zodiac paddle). If the state of decomposition of the animal allows, please also take photographs of the fluke (tail) and the dorsal fin (if present).

**Identification and data collection**
Recording species, including their latitude and longitude, and any other information can be of immense value, especially if photographs are included. Please send copies to IAATO at iaato@iaato.org.

**Helpful hints!**
- Reduce pollution from engines – in all close wildlife encounters, please ensure you are using 'clean running' engines, especially on small boats or Zodiacs.
- Polarising sunglasses can considerably enhance viewing of submerged/partially submerged marine animals and birds.
- Encourage the use of binoculars for viewing marine mammals and seabirds.

**Recommended field guides**
*Whales, Dolphins and Other Marine Mammals of the World* by Shirihai and Jarrett 2006.
*Birds of Chile, Antarctica and Southern Argentina* by Jaramillo, Burke and Beadle 2003.
*A Complete Guide to Antarctic Wildlife* by Shirihai and Jarrett 2002.
*National Audubon Guide to Marine Mammals of the World* by Folkiens et al. 2002.
*Seabirds: A Photographic Guide* by Peter Harrison, 1987.

These Guidelines are endorsed by the Sea Mammal Research Unit, Getty Marine Laboratory, University of St. Andrews. Guidelines revised by IAATO: 2007.

# Annex IV: Boot, Clothing and Equipment Decontamination Guidelines for Small Boat Operations

## International Association of Antarctica Tour Operators (IAATO)

### Introduction

While there is presently no conclusive evidence that tourists have introduced or transmitted diseases or any alien material in Antarctica, there is indirect and circumstantial evidence that raises concern. Furthermore, there is an acknowledged potential for visitors to be vectors of disease, both into and within the Antarctic ecosystem.

The Antarctic tourism industry, on its own initiative, recognised these concerns nearly a decade ago and began implementing procedures to address the possible introduction of alien organisms into Antarctica. In addition, IAATO commissioned a study designed to identify effective mitigation measures. As a result of these initiatives the following guidelines have been developed.

The guidelines are similar to the decontamination practices of those countries which protect themselves against the introduction of external diseases or alien organisms, and have been mandatory on all IAATO member vessels since 2001. The guidelines are regularly reviewed and updated as new information becomes available.

*Please note:* the term 'visitors' refers to all ship's crew, boat drivers, staff, guides and lecturers as well as to passengers.

### Procedures

*1. Pre-voyage information*

1.1 Visitors are to be advised that Antarctica is an isolated continent and believed to be largely free of introduced diseases and non-native species. We must ensure that it remains so.

1.2 Visitors are to be advised that all boots and clothing must be clean before joining the ship. Those who go trekking, tramping, backpacking, or farm visiting prior to the voyage must clean their boots, clothing and equipment thoroughly to remove all foreign material. Tripod feet and backpacks can also collect mud and seeds and should be checked regularly. Velcro attachments attract seeds and must be thoroughly checked and cleaned before departure to Antarctica.

*2. Pre-landing briefing*

2.1 Visitors need to be reminded that they must have clean boots, clothing and equipment before proceeding ashore. Facilities, known as the boot-washing station, will be available on deck for them to clean their equipment and their clothing and equipment will be checked thoroughly, preferably by a member of the ship's staff or crew, prior to their first landing.

*3. Boot-washing station*

3.1 This is a facility on the deck, at the head of

the gangway, or close to where passengers board the ship. It requires:

- running water and a hose – preferably high pressure to ensure complete removal of debris;
- drainage of water off the ship;
- scrubbing brush and / or coarse mat and shallow tray in which all debris can be scrubbed from boots and clothing;
- a second tray of water with disinfectant such as Virkon S[1];
- a member of staff or crew to assist visitors to inspect their boots and clothing for complete decontamination.

3.2 Before and after each landing all visitors going ashore must walk through the boot-washing station and ensure boots are free of debris and disinfected.

3.3 Boat crews may board via a different route to their passengers and should ensure they also complete the decontamination process.

*4. Landings*

4.1 Where possible, avoid walking in concentrations of organic material such as guano, seal placenta, or seal faeces, in order to avoid moving this material around the landing site.

4.2 Before boarding the small boat to return to the ship, debris – especially organic matter such as guano – should be washed off boots and clothing as much as is possible. A simple brush scrubber at the landing site should be used to clean boots before entering the Zodiac (or other small boat landing craft) at the end of the landing period. Do not forget to clean the debris off the brushes before returning to the ship.

Ensure that whatever touched the ground (backpacks in particular), boot cuffs, or exposed velcro are inspected, and cleaned before leaving the landing site. Seeds and other vegetation in the Sub-Antarctic islands can easily be transported if all visitors are not vigilant.

4.3 Where appropriate, clothing pockets can be turned out for vacuuming by staff on the ship as a precaution against transport of seeds.

4.4 On returning to the ship, boots, clothing and equipment must be cleaned thoroughly and disinfected at the boot-washing station. The disinfectant should not be rinsed off but allowed to dry thoroughly between landings

4.5 At the end of each landing, small boats should be inspected, and when necessary cleaned, to ensure that no foreign material is transported between sites.

1 As detailed in the IAATO *Introduction and Detection of Diseases in Antarctic Wildlife* and the paper *Identificiation of an Agent Suitable for Disinfecting Boots of Visitors*, it is recommended that a disinfectant be used at the boot washing station. To date, the disinfectant Virkon S is perceived as being the most effective. Be aware that careful handling of Virkon S is essential and instructions for use should be adhered to.

*5. Between landings*

5.1 Every effort must be made to ensure that boots and clothing dry out completely between landings. (Desiccation is an important mode of controlling some micro-organisms.) Visitors should be reminded in subsequent pre-landing briefings to inspect their boots and clothing to ensure that they are clean and no foreign material is present.

*IAATO Boot and Clothing Decontamination Guidelines*
Revised December 26, 2006

# Annex V: List of sites within the Antarctic Treaty area where special management conditions apply

The list is ordered first by region and within this from north to south, except East Antarctica which is listed clockwise from 0°E.

## Key to using table

| Site type | Entry allowed | Conditions to follow |
|---|---|---|
| Visitor Site Guidelines | Yes | Guidelines |
| Antarctic Specially Managed Area (ASMA) | Yes | Management plan and Code of Conduct |
| Antarctic Specially Protected Area (ASPA) | Only by special permit | Management plan |

## List of sites

| No. | Name | Text page | Map No. |
|---|---|---|---|
| **South Orkney Islands** | | | |
| 114 | Northern Coronation Island | 71 | 26 |
| 110 | Lynch Island | 71 | 26 |
| 109 | Moe Island | 71 | 26 |
| 111 | Southern Powell Island and adjacent islands | 72 | 27 |
| **South Shetland Islands** | | | |
| | Turret Point, King George Island | 40 | 7 |
| | Penguin Island, King George Island | 42 | 8 |
| 151 | Lions Rump, King George Island | 72 | 18 |
| 1 | Admiralty Bay, King George Island | 62 | 18 |
| 128 | Western shore of Admiralty Bay, King George Island | 72 | 18 |
| 132 | Potter Peninsula, '25 de Mayo' (King George) Island | 72 | 18 |
| 150 | Ardley Island, Maxwell Bay, King George Island | 73 | 29 |
| 125 | Fildes Peninsula, King George Island | 73 | 29 |
| 133 | Harmony Point, west coast of Nelson Island | 74 | 30 |
| 112 | Coppermine Peninsula, Robert Island | 74 | 31 |
| | Barrientos Island, Aitcho Islands | 45 | 9 |
| 144 | 'Chile Bay' (Discovery Bay), Greenwich Island | 74 | 31 |
| | Yankee Harbour, Greenwich Island | 47 | 10 |
| 149 | Cape Shirreff, Livingston Island | 74 | 32 |

| No. | Name | Text page | Map No. |
|-----|------|-----------|---------|
| **South Shetland Islands** *cont.* | | | |
| | Hannah Point, Livingston Island | 49 | 11 |
| 126 | Byers Peninsula, Livingston Island | 74 | 33 |
| 4 | Deception Island | 62 | 19 |
| 140 | Parts of Deception Island | 75 | 19 |
| 145 | Port Foster, Deception Island | 75 | 19 |
| 152 | Western Bransfield Strait off Low Island | 77 | 34 |

**Antarctic Peninsula**

| | | | |
|-----|------|-----------|---------|
| | Paulet Island, near Dundee Island | 34 | 4 |
| | Brown Bluff, Antarctic Sound | 36 | 5 |
| | Snow Hill, Nordenskjöld Hut | 38 | 6 |
| 148 | Mount Flora, Hope Bay | 77 | 36 |
| 134 | Cierva Point and offshore islands, Danco Coast | 77 | 37 |
| 153 | Eastern Dallmann Bay off Brabant Island, Palmer Archipelago | 77 | 34 |
| | Cuverville Island, Errera Channel | 52 | 13 |
| | Neko Harbour, Andvord Bay | 51 | 12 |
| | Goudier Island and Port Lockroy 'Base A', Wiencke Island | 54 | 14 |
| | Jougla Point, Wiencke Island | 57 | 15 |
| 146 | South Bay, Doumer Island, Palmer Archipelago | 77 | 38 |
| 139 | Biscoe Point, Anvers Island | 77 | 39 |
| 113 | Litchfield Island, Arthur Harbour, Anvers Island, Palmer Archipelago | 78 | 20 |
| | Pléneau Island, near Hovgaard Island | 58 | 16 |
| | Petermann Island, Penola Strait | 60 | 17 |
| 108 | Green Island, Berthelot Islands | 78 | 40 |
| 129 | Rothera Point, Adelaide Island | 78 | 41 |
| 117 | Avian Island, off Adelaide Island | 78 | 42 |
| 107 | Emperor Island, Dion Islands, Marguerite Bay | 78 | 42 |
| 115 | Lagotellerie Island, Marguerite Bay | 78 | 43 |
| 147 | Ablation Valley-Ganymede Heights, Alexander Island | 78 | 35 |

**West Antarctica from 45°W – 0°E**

| | | | |
|-----|------|-----------|---------|
| 119 | Davis Valley and Forlidas Pond, Dufek Massif | 80 | 21 |
| 5 | Amundsen-Scott South Pole Station, South Pole | | 21 |

**East Antarctica from 0°E – 155°E**

| | | | |
|-----|------|-----------|---------|
| 142 | Svarthamaren, Mühlig-Hofmannfjella, Dronning Maud Land | 80 | 21 |
| 163 | Dashkin Gangotri Glacier, Dronning Maud Land | 80 | 21 |

| No. | Name | Text page | Map No. |
|---|---|---|---|
| **East Antarctica from 0°E – 155°E** *cont.* | | | |
| 141 | 'Yukidori Valley', Langhovde, Lützow-Holmbukta | 80 | 21 |
| 101 | Taylor Rookery, Mac. Robertson Land | 80 | 44 |
| 102 | Rookery Islands, Holme Bay, Mac. Robertson Land | 80 | 44 |
| 164 | Scullin and Murray Monoliths, Mac. Robertson Land | 80 | 45 |
| 6 | Larsemann Hills, Prydz Bay, Princess Elizabeth Land | 68 | 23 |
| 143 | Marine Plain, Mule Peninsula, Vestfold Hills, Princess Elizabeth Land | 81 | 46 |
| 167 | Hawker Island, Vestfold Hills, Ingrid Christensen Coast, Princess Elizabeth Land | 81 | 46 |
| 127 | Haswell Island | 81 | 47 |
| 103 | Ardery Island and Odbert Island, Budd Coast | 81 | 48 |
| 135 | North-eastern Bailey Peninsula, Budd Coast, Wilkes Land | 81 | 48 |
| 136 | Clark Peninsula, Budd Coast, Wilkes Land | 82 | 48 |
| 160 | Frazier Islands, Wilkes Land | 82 | 48 |
| 120 | 'Pointe-Géologie Archipelago', Terre Adélie | 82 | 49 |
| 166 | Port-Martin, Terre Adélie | 82 | 21 |
| 3 | Cape Denison, Commonwealth Bay, George V Land | 67 | 22 |
| 162 | Mawson's Huts, Commonwealth Bay, George V Land | 82 | 22 |
| **Ross Sea** | | | |
| 104 | Sabrina Island, Balleny Islands | 82 | 50 |
| 159 | Cape Adare, Borchgrevink Coast, Northern Victoria Land | 83 | 24 |
| 106 | Cape Hallett, Victoria Land | 83 | 51 |
| 118 | Summit of Mount Melbourne, Victoria Land | 83 | 52 |
| 165 | Edmonson Point, Wood Bay, Victoria Land | 84 | 52 |
| 161 | Terra Nova Bay, Victoria Land | 84 | 53 |
| 154 | Botany Bay, Cape Geology, Victoria Land | 84 | 25 |
| 2 | McMurdo Dry Valleys, Southern Victoria Land | 69 | 25 |
| 123 | Barwick and Balham Valleys, Victoria Land | 84 | 25 |
| 138 | Linnaeus Terrace, Asgard Range, Victoria Land | 84 | 25 |
| 131 | Canada Glacier, Lake Fryxell, Taylor Valley, Victoria Land | 84 | 25 |
| 105 | Beaufort Island, McMurdo Sound | 85 | 25 |
| 124 | Cape Crozier, Ross Island | 85 | 25 |
| 156 | Lewis Bay, Mount Erebus, Ross Island | 85 | 25 |
| 130 | Tramway Ridge, Mount Erebus, Ross Island | 85 | 25 |
| 116 | New College Valley, Caughley Beach, Cape Bird, Ross Island | 85 | 25 |
| 121 | Cape Royds, Ross Island | 85 | 25 |

| No. | Name | Text page | Map No. |
|-----|------|-----------|---------|
| **Ross Sea** *cont.* | | | |
| 157 | Backdoor Bay, Cape Royds, Ross Island | 85 | 25 |
| 155 | Cape Evans, Ross Island | 85 | 25 |
| 158 | Hut Point, Ross Island | 85 | 25 |
| 122 | Arrival Heights, Hut Point Peninsula, Ross Island | 85 | 25 |
| 137 | Northwest White Island, McMurdo Sound | 85 | 25 |

# Annex VI: Historic Sites and Monuments within the Antarctic Treaty area

| No. | | Proposer | Latitude | Longitude |
|---|---|---|---|---|
| 1 | Flag mast erected in December 1965 at the South Geographical Pole by the First Argentine Overland Polar Expedition. | Argentina | 90°S | |
| 2 | Rock cairn and plaques at Syowa Station in memory of Shin Fukushima, who died in October 1960. | Japan | 69°00'S | 39°35'E |
| 3 | Rock cairn and plaque on Proclamation Island, Enderby Land, erected in January 1930 by Sir Douglas Mawson. | Australia | 65°51'S | 53°41'E |
| 4. | Bust of V.I. Lenin with a plaque in memory of the conquest of the Pole of Inaccessibility by Soviet Antarctic explorers in 1958. | Russia | 83°06'S | 54°58'E |
| 5. | Rock cairn and plaque at Cape Bruce, Mac. Robertson Land, erected in February 1931 by Sir Douglas Mawson. | Australia | 67°25'S | 60°47'E |
| 6. | Rock cairn at Walkabout Rocks, Vestfold Hills, Princess Elizabeth Land, erected in 1939 by Sir Hubert Wilkins. | Australia | 68°22'S | 78°33'E |
| 7. | Stone with plaque erected at Mirny Observatory in memory of Ivan Kharma who perished on official duties in 1956. | Russia | 66°33'S | 93°01'E |
| 8. | Metal monument / sledge at Mirny Observatory with plaque in memory of Anatoly Shcheglov who perished on official duties. | Russia | 66°33'S | 93°01'E |
| 9. | Cemetery on Buromskiy Island, whereSoviet, Czech and GDR citizens are buried, who perished on official duties in 1960. | Russia | 66°32'S | 93°01'E |
| 10. | Magnetic observatory at Dobrowolsky Station, Bunger Hills, with plaque in memory of the opening of Oasis Station in 1956. | Russia | 66°16'S | 100°45'E |
| 11. | Heavy tractor at Vostok Station with plaque in memory of the opening of the Station in 1957. | Russia | 78°28'S | 106°48'E |
| 12. | De-listed | Australia | 67°00'S | 142°42'E |
| 13. | De-listed | Australia | 67°00'S | 142°42'E |
| 14. | Site of ice cave, Inexpressible Island, Terra Nova Bay, built March 1912 by British Antarctic Expedition, 1910-13. | New Zealand | 74°54'S | 163°43'E |
| 15. | Hut at Cape Royds, Ross Island, built by British Antarctic Expedition 1907-09. Incorporated within ASPA No. 157. | New Zealand/ UK | 77°33'S | 166°10'E |
| 16. | Hut at Cape Evans, Ross Island, built by British Antarctic Expedition 1910-1913. Incorporated within ASPA No. 155. | New Zealand/ UK | 77°38'S | 166°24'E |

| No. | | Proposer | Latitude | Longitude |
|-----|---|----------|----------|-----------|
| 17. | Cross at Cape Evans, Ross Island, erected in memory of 3 members who died on the Imperial Trans-Antarctic Expedition (1914-1916). Incorporated within ASPA No. 155. | New Zealand/ UK | 77°38'S | 166°24'E |
| 18. | Hut at Hut Point, Ross Island, built by the British Antarctic Expedition of 1901-04. Site incorporated within ASPA No. 158. | New Zealand/ UK | 77°50'S | 166°37'E |
| 19. | Cross at Hut Point, Ross Island, erected by the British Antarctic Expedition (1901-04) in memory of George Vince. | New Zealand/ UK | 77°50'S | 166°37'E |
| 20. | Cross on Observation Hill, Ross Island, erected by British Antarctic Expedition (1910-13) in memory of Scott's party which perished on the return from the South Pole in March 1912. | New Zealand/ UK | 77°51'S | 166°41'E |
| 21. | Remains of stone hut at Cape Crozier, Ross Island, constructed by Wilson's party of the British Antarctic Expedition (1910-13). | New Zealand | 77°31'S | 169°22'E |
| 22. | Two huts built by British Antarctic Expedition (1898-1900), and hut built in 1911 by Scott's Northern Party at Cape Adare. Incorporated within ASPA No. 159. | New Zealand/ UK | 71°18'S | 170°12'E |
| 23. | Grave at Cape Adare of Norwegian biologist Nicolai Hanson, member of the British Antarctic Expedition (1898-1900). | New Zealand/ UK | 71°17'S | 170°13'E |
| 24. | Rock cairn, known as 'Amundsen's cairn', on Mount Betty, Queen Maud Range erected by Roald Amundsen on 6 January 1912, on his way back to Framheim from the South Pole. | Norway | 85°11'S | 163°45'W |
| 25. | De-listed | | | |
| 26. | Abandoned installations of Argentine Station 'General San Martin' on Barry Island, Marguerite Bay, built in 1951. | Argentina | 68°08'S | 67°08'W |
| 27. | Cairn with a replica of a lead plaque erected on Petermann Island, in 1909 by Charcot on the 2nd French expedition. | Argentina/ France/ UK | 65°10'S | 64°09'W |
| 28. | Rock cairn at Port Charcot, Booth Island, with wooden pillar and plaque inscribed with the names of the 1st French expedition led by Charcot which wintered here in 1904 aboard Le Français. | Argentina | 65°03'S | 64°01'W |
| 29. | Lighthouse named 'Primero de Mayo' erected on Lambda Island, Melchior Islands, by Argentina in 1942. This was the first Argentine lighthouse in the Antarctic. | Argentina | 64°18'S | 62°59'W |
| 30. | Shelter at Paradise Harbour erected in 1950 near the Chilean Base to honour Gabriel Gonzalez Videla. | Chile | 64°49'S | 62°51'W |
| 31. | De-listed. | | | |

| No. | | Proposer | Latitude | Longitude |
|-----|---|----------|----------|-----------|
| 32. | Concrete monolith erected in 1947, near Capitán Arturo Prat Base on Greenwich Island, South Shetland Islands. | Chile | 62°28'S | 59°40'W |
| 33. | Shelter, cross and plaque near Capitán Arturo Prat Base (Chile), Greenwich Island, in memory of L-C. González Pacheco, who died in 1960 while in charge of the station. | Chile | 62°29'S | 59°40'W |
| 34. | Bust at Capitán Arturo Prat Base (Chile), Greenwich Island, of the Chilean naval hero Arturo Prat, erected in 1947. | Chile | 62°50'S | 59°41'W |
| 35. | Wooden cross and statue of the Virgin of Carmen erected in 1947 near Capitán Arturo Prat Base (Chile), Greenwich Island. | Chile | 62°29'S | 59°40'W |
| 36. | Replica of a metal plaque erected by Eduard Dallmann at Potter Cove, King George Island. | Argentina/ UK | 62°14'S | 58°39'W |
| 37. | Statue erected in 1948 at General Bernardo O'Higgins Base (Chile), Trinity Peninsula, of Bernardo O'Higgins. | Chile | 63°19'S | 57°54'W |
| 38. | Wooden hut on Snow Hill Island built in 1902 by members of Nordenskjöld's Swedish South Polar Expedition. | Argentina/ UK | 64°22'S | 56°59'W |
| 39. | Stone hut at Hope Bay, Trinity Peninsula, built in January 1903 by a party of the Swedish South Polar Expedition. | Argentina/ UK | 63°24'S | 56°59'W |
| 40. | Commemorative bust of General San Martin, and other items at Base 'Esperanza', Hope Bay, erected by Argentina in 1955. | Argentina | 63°24'S | 56°59'W |
| 41. | Stone hut on Paulet Island built in 1903 by survivors of the wrecked vessel Antarctic under Captain Larsen, members of Nordenskjöld's Swedish South Polar Expedition. | Argentina/ UK | 63°34'S | 55°45'W |
| 42. | Scotia Bay, Laurie Island, South Orkney Islands: stone hut built in 1903 by Scottish Antarctic Expedition; Argentine hut and observatory built 1905; graveyard dating from 1903. | Argentina | 60°46'S | 44°40'W |
| 43. | Cross erected in 1955 at Belgrano I Station (Argentina) and subsequently moved to Belgrano II Station, Coats Land. | Argentina | 77°52'S | 34°37'W |
| 44. | Plaque erected at Indian station 'Dakshin Gangotri', Princess Astrid Kyst, Dronning Maud Land. | India | 70°45'S | 11°38'E |
| 45. | Plaque on Metchnikoff Point, Brabant Island to commemorate the first landing on Brabant Island by the Belgian Antarctic Expedition (1897-99). | Belgium | 64°02'S | 62°34'W |
| 46. | All the buildings and installations of Port-Martin base, Terre Adélie constructed in 1950 by the 3rd French expedition, partly destroyed by fire in January 1952. | France | 66°49'S | 141°24'E |
| 47. | Wooden building on the Ile des Pétrels, Terre Adélie, where men overwintered in 1952 following the fire at Port Martin Base. | France | 66°40'S | 140°01'E |

| No. | | Proposer | Latitude | Longitude |
|-----|--|----------|----------|-----------|
| 48. | Cross on Ile des Pétrels, Terre Adélie, as a memorial to André Prudhomme who disappeared in a blizzard in 1959. | France | 66°40'S | 140°01'E |
| 49. | Pillar erected by 1st Polish Antarctic Expedition at Dobrolowski Station to measure acceleration due to gravity in January 1959. | Poland | 66°16'S | 100°45'E |
| 50. | Plaque bearing Polish Eagle 1st Polish Antarctic marine research expedition in February 1976. Mounted on a cliff facing Maxwell Bay, Fildes Peninsula, King George Island. | Poland | 62°12'S | 59°01'W |
| 51. | The grave of Wlodzimierz Puchalski, surmounted by an iron cross, south of Arctowski station on King George Island. | Poland | 62°13'S | 58°28'W |
| 52. | Monolith to commemorate establishment of 'Great Wall Station' (China) on Fildes Peninsula, King George Island. | China | 62°13'S | 58°58'W |
| 53. | Bust of Captain Luis Alberto Pardo, monolith and plaques on Point Wild, Elephant Island, South Shetland Islands, celebrating rescue of the survivors of the British ship Endurance by the Chilean Navy cutter Yelcho. | Chile | 61°03'S | 54°50'W |
| 54. | Richard E. Byrd Historic Monument, erected at McMurdo Station in 1965. | USA | 77°51'S | 166°40'E |
| 55. | Buildings and artefacts at East Base, Stonington Island. The size of the historic area is approximately 1000 metres (N-S) x 500 metres (E-W). | USA | 68°11'S | 67°00'W |
| 56. | The remains and immediate environs of Waterboat Point hut, Danco Coast. Situated near Videla Station (Chile). | Chile/ UK | 64°49'S | 62°51'W |
| 57. | Plaque at Yankee Harbour, Greenwich Island, commemorating Capt. MacFarlane, who explored the Antarctic Peninsula in 1820. | Chile/ UK | 62°32'S | 59°45'W |
| 58. | De-listed. | | | |
| 59. | Cairn on Half Moon Beach, Cape Shirreff, Livingston Island, and a plaque opposite San Telmo Islets commemorating loss of the San Telmo in 1819; incorporated within ASPA No. 149. | Chile/ Spain/ Peru | 62°28'S | 60°46'W |
| 60. | Wooden plaque and cairn placed in 1903 at Penguins Bay, Seymour Island, by crew of the Argentinian vessel Uruguay where they met members of Nordenskjöld's Swedish expedition. | Argentina | 64°16'S | 56°39'W |
| 61. | 'Base A' at Port Lockroy, Goudier Island, off Wiencke Island; was a key monitoring site during IGY of 1957/58. | UK | 64°49'S | 63°29'W |
| 62. | 'Base F (Wordie House)' on Winter Island, Argentine Islands. Of importance as an example of an early British scientific base. | UK | 65°15'S | 64°16'W |

| No. | | Proposer | Latitude | Longitude |
|---|---|---|---|---|
| 63. | 'Base Y' on Horseshoe Island, Marguerite Bay. Noteworthy as a relatively unaltered and completely equipped British scientific base of the late 1950s. 'Blaiklock', the refuge hut nearby, is considered an integral part of the base. | UK | 67°48'S | 67°18'W |
| 64. | 'Base E' on Stonington Island, Marguerite Bay, western Graham Land. Of importance in the early period of exploration and later British Antarctic Survey (BAS) history of the 1960s and 1970s. | UK | 68°11'S | 67°00'W |
| 65. | Message post, Svend Foyn Island, Possession Islands. A pole with a box attached was placed on the island in 1895 during the whaling expedition of the ship Antarctic. | New Zealand/ Norway/ UK | 71°56'S | 171°05'W |
| 66. | Prestrud's Cairn, Scott Nunataks, Alexandra Mountains. Erected during the Norwegian Antarctic Expedition of 1910-1912. | New Zealand/ Norway/ UK | 77°11'S | 154°32'W |
| 67. | Rock shelter, 'Granite House', Cape Geology, Granite Harbour, constructed during the British Antarctic Expedition of 1910-1913. Incorporated within ASPA No. 154. | New Zealand/ Norway/ UK | 77°00'S | 162°32'E |
| 68. | Site of depot at Hells Gate Moraine, Inexpressible Island, Terra Nova Bay, placed by British Antarctic Expedition (1910-1913). | New Zealand/ Norway/ UK | 74°52'S | 163°50'E |
| 69. | Message post at Cape Crozier, Ross Island, erected in 1902 by Scott's Discovery Expedition (1901-04). Incorporated within ASPA No. 124. | New Zealand/ Norway/ UK | 77°27'S | 169°16'E |
| 70. | Message post at Cape Wadworth, Coulman Island. A metal cylinder nailed to a red pole 8 m ASL placed by Scott in 1902. | New Zealand/ Norway/ UK | 73°19'S | 169°47'E |
| 71. | Whalers Bay, Deception Island, comprises all pre-1970 remains at Whalers Bay, including from the whaling period 1906-12; the Norwegian Whaling Station established in 1912 and associated artefacts; the site of a cemetery; and remains of British scientific and mapping activity (1944-1969). | Chile/ Norway | 62°59'S | 60°34'W |
| 72. | Mikkelsen Cairn, Tryne Islands, Vestfold Hills. A rock cairn and a wooden mast erected by members of the Norwegian ship Thorshavn including Caroline Mikkelsen, the first woman to set foot on East Antarctica. | Australia/ Norway | 68°22'S | 78°24'E |
| 73. | Memorial Cross for the 1979 Mount Erebus aircraft crash victims, Lewis Bay, Ross Island, erected as a mark of respect and in remembrance of those who died in the tragedy. | New Zealand | 77°25'S | 167°27'E |
| 74. | The un-named cove on the SW coast of Elephant Island, including the foreshore and the intertidal area, in which the wreckage of a large wooden sailing vessel is located. | UK | 61°14'S | 55°22'W° |

| No. | | Proposer | Latitude | Longitude |
|-----|---|----------|----------|-----------|
| 75. | The A Hut of Scott Base, being the only existing Trans Antarctic Expedition 1956/1957 building, Ross Island. | New Zealand | 77°51'S | 166°46'E |
| 76. | The ruins of Pedro Aguirre Cerda Station (Chile), Deception Island, destroyed by volcanic eruptions in 1967 and 1969. | Chile | 62°59'S | 60°40'W |
| 77. | Cape Denison, Commonwealth Bay, including Boat Harbour and the historic artefacts contained within its waters. Incorporated within ASMA No. 3 and also designated as ASPA No. 162 | Australia | 67°00'30''S | 142°39'40''E |
| 78. | Memorial plaque at India Point, Humboldt Mountains, central Dronning Maud Land, erected in memory of Indian personnel who lost their lives in 1990. | India | 71°45'08''S | 11°12'30''E |
| 79. | Lillie Marleen Hut, Mt. Dockery, Northern Victoria Land, erected to support the work of the German Antarctic Northern Victoria Land Expedition (GANOVEX I) of 1979/1980. | Germany | 71°12'S | 164°31'E |
| 80. | Amundsen's Tent, erected at 90° by Amundsen's party on arrival at the South Pole in 1911. The tent is buried underneath snow and ice in the vicinity of the South Pole. | Norway | In the vicinity of 90°S | |
| 81. | Rocher du Débarquement (Landing Rock) is a small island where Dumont D'Urville landed in 1840 when he discovered Terre Adélie. | France | 66° 36. 30'S | 140° 03.85'E |
| 82. | Monument to the Antarctic Treaty and Plaque located on Fildes Peninsula, King George Island. Commemorates the Signatories to the Antarctic Treaty and successive International Polar Years (1882-1883, 1932-1933 and 2007-2008). | Chile | 62°12' 01''S | 58°57'41''W |

Source: Abridged from Antarctic Protected Areas Information Archive:
http://cep.ats.aq/cep/apa/index.html

# Annex VII: Information resources

There is a host of information available on the internet, so if you have access, we suggest you first look at the IAATO website www.iaato.org and download the following essential documents for reference when cruising in Antarctic waters:

## IAATO environmental protection guidelines

- IAATO Marine Wildlife Watching Guidelines
- IAATO Boot and Clothing Decontamination Guidelines
- IAATO Introduction and Detection of Diseases in Antarctic Wildlife
- IAATO Emergency Contingency Planning

## Antarctic Treaty environmental protection guidelines

- Guidance for Visitors to the Antarctic
- Recommendation XVIII-1 for Visitors in English, Spanish, French, Russian, German, Japanese, Italian, Chinese, Dutch
- Protocol on Environmental Protection to the Antarctic Treaty (1991) – known as the Environmental Protocol 1991. See www.ats.aq/archive.php
- Guidelines for the Operation of Aircraft near Concentrations of Birds in the Antarctic (including microlites, gyrocopters etc). See www.comnap.aq/publications/guidelines
- Guidelines on Contingency Planning, Insurance and Other Matters for Tourist and Other Non-Governmental Activities in the Antarctic Treaty area

- Guidelines For Ships Operating in Arctic and Antarctic Ice Covered Waters

## Seasonal documents

- IAATO vessel call data and ship schedules (usually available October)
- Post-Visit Report Forms

## Site specific guidelines and resources

- IAATO Site Specific Guidelines on the Antarctic Peninsula
- Antarctic Treaty Visitor Site Guidelines agreed by the Treaty Parties. See www.ats.aq under 'Topics' > 'Other'
- Deception Island Management Plan. See www.ats.aq/28atcm/buscador.php?pagina=2 for the official documents, which is also available with additional information at www.deceptionisland.aq

## Procedures for visiting stations

- Procedures for Tourist or Non-Governmental Expeditions Requesting a Visit to BAS Research Stations or Historic Sites are available at www.antarctica.ac.uk/about_antarctica/tourism/index.php

## Domestic legislation

- A complete list of domestic legislation is included in ATCMXXV Information Paper 85 *Regulatory Mechanisms That Address Antarctic Tourism*
- Other countries such as Argentina, Australia, Germany, Japan, New Zealand, United Kingdom, the Netherlands all have domestic legislation

- *Polar Updates*, compiled by David Rootes and Wiz Pasteur (published by Poles Apart, Cambridge), summarises the environmental legislation relating to Antarctica and the sub-Antarctic islands for all signatories to Antarctic Treaty. This useful reference, which is periodically updated, includes details of visitor requirements, environmental documentation, permits required, fees and administrative costs, and contact agencies. Contact www.polesapart.org for copies.

### Publications

- The British Hydrographic Office's *The Antarctic Pilot* contains a wealth of information on many aspects of polar navigation, with descriptions of anchorages (usually for large vessels though, rather than yachts), coastlines and ice conditions, as well as information on wildlife, weather and history. Navigation charts for the Antarctic are produced by several countries. Generally, the best charts for any particular area are produced by those countries with stations nearby, and many of them are listed in *The Antarctic Pilot.*

- Jeff Rubin's *Antarctica* (Lonely Planet Publications, 2005) is one of the most comprehensive information books written about Antarctica.

- Other useful books include: Ron Naveen's *The Oceanites Site Guide to the Antarctic Peninsula* (Chevy Chase: Oceanites, 1997; 2nd edition 2005); *The Greenpeace Book of Antarctica* (New York: Doubleday, 1988; Readers Digest's *Antarctic: The Extraordinary History of Man's Conquest of the Frozen Continent* (Sydney: Readers Digest, 1990); Hadoram Shirihai's *The Complete Guide to Antarctic Wildlife* (Princeton University Press, 2002); David McGonigal and Lynn Woodworth's *Antarctica: The Complete Story* (The Five Mile Press, 2001); Bernard Stonehouse's *Antarctica from South America* (Originator Publishing, 2006) and *The Last Continent: Discovering Antarctica* (SCP Books, 2000); Beau Riffenburgh's (ed) *The Encyclopedia of the Antarctic* (Routledge, 2007) is a mine of information.

- Handbooks produced by national governmental organisations are a useful source of information, for example *A Visitor's Introduction To The Antarctic And Its Environment* published by the British Antarctic Survey, Madingley Road, Cambridge CB3 OET, United Kingdom, and also by the Australian Antarctic Division, Kingston, Tasmania 7050, Australia.

- A Wildlife Awareness Manual for the Antarctic Peninsula / South Shetland Islands / South Orkney Islands region developed to meet the needs of helicopter pilots provides practical information also of more general utility. In addition to the 156 colour maps showing the location of breeding wildlife (penguins, petrels, shags, fulmars, fur seals), information is also included on scientific stations, protected areas and historic sites. Reference: Harris, C.M. (ed) 2006. *Wildlife Awareness Manual: Antarctic Peninsula, South Shetland Islands, South Orkney Islands.* 1st edn. Wildlife Information Publication No. 1. Prepared for UK Foreign

& Commonwealth Office and HMS
*Endurance.* Published by *Environmental
Research & Assessment,* Cambridge (www.
era.gs/resources/wam).

For a complete selection of new and second-
hand polar books, contact:
Bluntisham Books, Oak House, East Street,
Bluntisham, Huntingdon, United Kingdom,
PE17 3LS, contact@bluntisham.org
Polar Exploration Books, c/o P. Walcott, 60
Sunnybank Road, Sutton Coldfield, West
Midlands, B73 5RJ, UK.

For publications when in South Atlantic
Antarctic gateway ports, try:
El Boutique del Libro, Ushuaia, Argentina.
The Jetty Centre and Capstan Gift Shop,
Stanley, Falkland Islands.

### Internet resources
The Antarctic Treaty and the Protocol on
Environmental Protection to the Antarctic
Treaty are available through the Antarctic
Treaty Secretariat at: www.ats.aq/archive.php

Antarctic Treaty Secretariat: www.ats.aq
Antarctic Protected Areas Information
Archive: cep.ats.aq/cep/apa/index.html
Bluntisham Books, polar bookseller:
www.bluntishambooks.co.uk
Committee for Environmental Protection:
cep.ats.aq/cep/
Council of Managers of National Antarctic
Programs: www.comnap.aq
Deception Island, ASMA No. 4:
www.deceptionisland.aq
Environmental Research & Assessment:
www.era.gs

Falkland Islands Government:
www.falklands.gov.fk
Heard Island:
www.heardisland.aq
International Association of Antarctica Tour
Operators:
www.iaato.org
International Maritime Organization (IMO):
www.imo.org
Macquarie Island, Tasmanian Parks and
Wildlife Service:
www.parks.tas.gov.au/macquarie/index.
html
Oceanites Site Guide to the Antarctic
Peninsula:
www.oceanites.org
Patagonia & Tierra del Fuego Nautical
Guide:
www.capehorn-pilot.com
Polar Updates:
www.polesapart.org
Sailing in Falklands waters:
www.falklandsailing.com
Scientific Committee on Antarctic Research:
www.scar.org
Southern Ocean Cruising:
www.era.gs/resources/soc
South Georgia Government:
www.sgisland.org
South Georgia Surveys: www.
southgeorgiasurveys.org
UK Hydrographic Office – The Antarctic
Pilot:
www.ukho.gov.uk
Wildlife Awareness Manual – Antarctic
Peninsula:
www.era.gs/resources/wam
World Heritage List: http://whc.unesco.
org/en/list

**National Antarctic Programmes and academic institutions**

Alfred Wegener Institute (Germany):
www.awi.de/en/home/

Antarctica New Zealand:
www.antarcticanz.govt.nz

Australian Antarctic Division:
www.aad.gov.au

British Antarctic Survey:
www.antarctica.ac.uk

Byrd Polar Research Center:
www-bprc.mps.ohio-state.edu

French National Antarctic Programme:
www.institut-polaire.fr

Gateway Antarctica, University of
Canterbury:
www.anta.canterbury.ac.nz

Institute of Antarctic and Southern Ocean
Studies:
fcms.its.utas.edu.au/scieng/iasos/index.
asp

Instituto Antártico Argentino:
www.dna.gov.ar

Instituto Antártico Chileno (INACH):
www.inach.cl

Norwegian Polar Institute:
npiweb.npolar.no

Office of Polar Programs, National Science
Foundation, United States of America:
www.nsf.gov/dir/index.jsp?org=opp

Italian National Antarctic Programme:
www.pnra.it

Scott Polar Research Institute:
www.spri.cam.ac.uk

South African National Antarctic
Programme:
www.sanap.org.za

United States Antarctic Program:
www.usap.gov

**National contact details for Antarctica**

**Australia**

The Assistant Secretary, Legal Branch
Department of Foreign Affairs and Trade
The Rg Casey Building
John McEwen Crescent, Barton ACT 0221
Tel: (+61) 2 6261 9111
Fax: (+61) 2 6261 2144

The Director
Australian Antarctic Division
Channel Highway, Kingston, Tasmania 7050
Tel: (+61) 3 6232 3200
Fax: (+61) 3 6232 3215

**Argentina**

Dirección de Antártida
Ministerio de Relaciones Exteriores
Comercio Internacional y Culto
Reconquista 1088 - Piso 10
Buenos Aires, Argentina
Tel: (+54) 1311 1801
Fax: (+54) 1311 1660

Dirección Nacional del Antártico
Instituto Antártico Argentino
Cerrito 1248, Buenos Aires
Tel: (+54) 1813 7807
Tel: (+54) 1812 1689
Fax: (+54) 1 1812 2039

**Belgium**

Ministère des Affaires Etrangères
Service Environnement et Développement
Durable
Rue des Petits Carmes 15, Brussels
Tel: (+32) 2501 3712/06
Fax: (+32) 2501 3703

Federal Office for Scientific, Technical
  and Cultural Affairs (OSTC)
Rue de la Science 8
Brussels
Tel: (+32) 2238 3609
Tel: (+32) 2238 3411
Fax: (+32) 2230 5912

## Canada
Director-General
Multi-Lateral Affairs Division
Environment Canada
Ottawa
Canada K1A 0E4
Tel (819) 994 5687

## Chile
Ministerio de Relaciones Exteriores
Dirección de Medio Ambiente
Departamento Antartica
Catedral # 1158
Santiago
Tel: (+56) 2 679 4379
Fax: (+56) 2 672 5071

Instituto Antártico Chileno
Romulo Correa 375
Plaza Muñoz Gamero 1055
Punta Arenas
Tel: (+56) 61 298 100

## France
Administration des Terres Australes
  et Antarctiques Françaises
  (T.A.A.F.)
Rue des Renaudes
Paris
Tel: (+33) 4053 4677
Fax: (+33) 4766 9123

Ministère des Affaires Etrangères
Direction des Affaires Juridiques
Sous Direction de droit de la mer, des
  Pêches et de l'Antarctique
Quai d'Orsay 75007
Paris
Tel: (+33) 4753 5331 ext. 4386 / 5331 /
  5325
Fax: (+33) 4753 9495

## Germany
Auswärtiges Amt
Referat 504, Postfach 1148
Bonn
Tel: (+49) 228-172997
Fax: (+49) 228-173784

Alfred-Wegener-Institut
Columbusstrasse
Bremerhaven
Tel: (+49) 471-4831-0
Fax: (+49) 471-4831-149

## Italy
Ministero Degli Affari Esteri
Direzione Generale Delle Relazioni
  Culturali (DGRC)
Ufficio VII, Ple Delle Farnesina 1 - 00194
  Roma
Tel: (+39) 6 3691 4057 / 3691 4061
Fax: (+39) 6 323 6239

Energy and Environment Agency
  (ENEA)
Progetto Antartide
S P Anguillarese, 301
Roma A.D.
Tel: (+39) 6 3048 4939
Fax: (+39) 6 3048 4893

**The Netherlands**
DES-ET
Ministry of Foreign Affairs
P O Box 20061
EB The Hague
Tel: (+31) 70 348 4971
Fax: (+31) 70 348 4412

**New Zealand**
Antarctic Policy Unit
Ministry of Foreign Affairs and Trade
Private Bay 18-901
Wellington
Tel: (+64) 4 439 8000
Fax: (+64) 4 439 8511

Antarctica New Zealand
Private Bag 4745
Christchurch 8140
Tel: (+64) 3 358 0200
Fax: (+64) 3 358 0211

**Spain**
Dirección General de Relaciones
    Culturales y Cientificas
Ministerio de Asuntos Exteriores
Atocha, 3
28012 Madrid
Tel: (+34) 91 379 9559
Fax: (+34) 91 531 9366

**United Kingdom**
Polar Regions Unit
Overseas Territories Directorate
Foreign and Commonwealth Office
King Charles Street
London SW1A 2AH
Tel: (+44) 207 7008 2717
Fax: (+44) 207 7008 2086

Environmental Officer
British Antarctic Survey
Madingley Road, High Cross
Cambridge CB3 0ET
Tel: (+44) 1223 221 400
Fax: (+44) 1223 362 616

**United States of America**
The Director
Office of Oceans Affairs
OES/OA, Room 5805
Department of State
Washington, DC 20520-7818
Tel: (+1) (202) 647 3262
Fax: (+1) (202) 647 1106

Office of Polar Programs
Room 755
National Science Foundation
4201 Wilson Boulevard
Arlington, VA 22230
Tel: (+1) (703) 292-8030
Fax (+1) (703) 292-9081

# Annex VIII: Yacht voyages to the Southern Ocean

This is a list of yachts – large and small – that have sailed to the Antarctic and sub-Antarctic region, their skippers and crew, the islands or regions visited, and the books and films in which the voyage was recorded. Where no book was published, we have listed magazines or reports that refer to the voyage. The year of each summer visit is expressed as the austral summer period, taken to include the end of one year and the beginning of the next. For those yachts that have wintered-over, the time period includes the two summers either side of the winter.

Modern yacht cruises and expeditions to the Southern Oceans could well be said to have began with Joshua Slocum's circumnavigation with the *Spray* in 1895 – 1898 during which time he sailed the Chilean Canals and coast of Tierra del Fuego.

At the beginning of the 20th century, other vessels ventured further south still. Some were no bigger than today's private yachts. They served as logistic support vessels for non-governmental, privately-funded expeditions that explored, mapped and studied those then little-known latitudes. Although these expeditions and their crews were motivated by scientific research and exploration rather than recreational pursuits, they were nonetheless the forerunners of today's yachts, many of which are also privately funded and on occasions motivated by scientific research as well as adventure.Entries for the period 1992-2000 are from R. K. Headland's unpublished

revision (2001) of *Antarctic Chronology* (1989). The authors would welcome corrections and any additional information regarding regions visited and resulting publications – emails to sallyponcet@horizon.co.fk.

**1902-03:**
*MORNING* – Britain – Captain W. Colbeck and crew – McMurdo Sound in the Ross Sea.

**1903-04:**
*MORNING* – Britain – Captain W. Colbeck and crew – McMurdo Sound and Winter Quarters Bay in the Ross Sea.
Doorly, G.S. *1936. In the Wake.* Robertson & Mullens Ltd.

**1903-05:** WINTER-OVER
*FRANÇAIS* – France – Jean-Baptiste Charcot, E. Cholet (skipper) and crew.
*1903-04:* Tierra del Fuego, Antarctic Peninsula.
*1904 :* WINTERED at Booth Island, Antarctic Peninsula.
*1904-05:* Antarctic Peninsula.
Charcot, J-B, *1906. Le 'Français' Au Pole Sud.* Flammarion.

**1907-09:** WINTER-OVER
*JEAN-BAPTISTE CHARCOT-* France – Raymond and Henri Rallier Du Baty and crew – Îles Kerguelen from March *1908* to June *1909.*
*1907-08:* Îles Kerguelen.
*1908 :* WINTERED at Îles Kerguelen.
*1908-09:* Îles Kerguelen.

Rallier Du Baty, R. *1910. Fifteen Thousand Miles in a Ketch.* Thomas Nelson and Sons Ltd.

**1908-10:** WINTER-OVER
*POURQUOI-PAS?* – Jean Baptiste Charcot, E. Cholet (skipper) and crew.
1908-09: Tierra del Fuego, South Shetlands, Antarctic Peninsula.
1909 : WINTERED at Petermann Island, Antarctic Peninsula.
Charcot, J-B. 1910. *Le Pourquoi Pas?' dans L'Antarctique.* Flammarion.

**1912-14:** WINTER-OVER
*LA CURIEUSE-* France – Raymond Rallier Du Baty and crew.
1912-13: Îles Kerguelen.
1913: WINTERED at Îles Kerguelen.
1913-14: Îles Kerguelen.
Rallier Du Baty, R. 1911. *Le Voyage de* la *'Curieuse'* in Volume 37 of *La Geographie.*

**1934-37:** WINTER-OVER
*PENOLA* – Britain – John Rymill, R. Ryder (captain) and crew.
1934-35: Falkland Islands, Antarctic Peninsula.
1935: WINTERED at Argentine Islands, Antarctic Peninsula.
1935-36: Antarctic Peninsula, South Shetlands, Falkland Islands.
1936: Falkland Islands, South Georgia.
1936-37: South Georgia, Falkland Islands, South Shetlands, Antarctic Peninsula.
Rymill, J. 1939. *Southern Lights.* Travel Book Club.
Film: *The British Graham Land Expedition.*

**1946-47:**
*ALBATROSS-* Britain – Niall Rankin and crew

– South Georgia.
Rankin, N. 1951. *Antarctic Isle.* Collins.

**1959-60:**
*MISCHIEF* – Britain – Harold 'Bill' Tilman and crew – Îles Crozet and Kerguelen.
Tilman, H W. 1961. *Mischief Among The Penguins.* Hollis and Carter.
*PATANELA* – Australia – Alan Powell and crew – Macquarie Island.

**1964-65:**
*PATANELA* – Australia – Harold 'Bill' Tilman (skipper), Warwick Deacock and crew – Heard Island and Îles Kerguelen.
Tilman, H W. 1966. *Mostly Mischief.* Hollis and Carter.
Temple, P. 1966. *The Sea and the Snow.* Cassell.

**1966-67:**
*MISCHIEF* – Britain – Harold 'Bill' Tilman and crew – South Shetlands and South Georgia.
Tilman, H. W. 1986. *Mischief Goes South.* Hollis & Carter.

**1968-69:**
*MARAVAL* – New Zealand – Neil Brown and crew – Auckland Islands.

**1970-71:**
*AWAHNEE II* – United States – Bob & Nancy Griffiths and crew – Campbell Island, South Shetlands, South Orkneys, Antarctic Peninsula.
*DAMIEN* – France – Jérôme Poncet and Gerard Janichon – Tierra del Fuego, South Georgia.
Janichon, G. 1973. *Damien: Du Spitsberg au Cap Horn.* Editions Arthaud.
*SAN GUISEPPE DUE* – Italy – Antonio Ajmone-Cat and crew – Falkland Islands, South Shetlands.

**1971-72:**

*DAMIEN* – France – Jérôme Poncet and Gérard Janichon – Îles Kerguelen and Crozet, Heard and Macquarie Islands.

Janichon, G 1974. *Damien: Icebergs et Mers Australes.* Editions Arthaud.

**1972-73:**

*DAMIEN* – France – Jérôme Poncet and Gérard Janichon – Antarctic Peninsula, South Shetlands, South Georgia.

Janichon, G 1975. *Damien: L'Antarctique à la Voile.* Editions Arthaud.

Film: *Icebergs et Mers Australes.*

*KETIGA* – New Zealand – Gerry Clark – Auckland, Campbell, Antipodes and Bounty Islands.

Clark, G. 1973. April issue of New Zealand *Sea Spray* magazine.

*MARAVAL* – New Zealand – Neil Brown and crew – Auckland Island and Campbell Island.

*ST. MICHAEL* – New Zealand – Nicholas, John and Sam Atkinson – Auckland Island.

Yaldwyn J. 1975. *Preliminary Results of The Auckland Island Expedition 1972-73.* Department of Lands and Survey New Zealand.

**1972-74:**

*ICE-BIRD* – Australia – David Lewis.

1972-73: Antarctic Peninsula (Palmer Station).

WINTER 1973: yacht left at Palmer Station.

1973-74: Antarctic Peninsula and South Orkneys.

Lewis, D. 1975. *Ice Bird.* William Collins & Sons Co. Ltd.

**1973-74:**

*SAN GUISEPPE DUE* – Italy – Giovanni Ajmone-Cat and crew – Tierra del Fuego, Falkland

Islands, Antarctic Peninsula, South Orkneys, South Georgia.

**1974-75:**

*VALYA* – New Zealand – Anthony Lealand and crew – Campbell Island.

**1975-76:**

*GEDANIA* – Poland – Darius Gullet Bogucki and crew – Falkland Islands, South Shetlands, Antarctic Peninsula.

*TRISMUS* – Belgium – Patrick Van God & Wendy Farr – Tierra del Fuego, South Shetlands, Antarctic Peninsula, Faraday, Port Charcot, Palmer Station, Port Lockroy, Dorian Cove, Melchior.

Van God, P. 1976. *Pour L'Aventure.* Editions Arthaud.

Film: *L'Antarctique à la Voile.*

**1976-77:**

*WAVEWALKER* – Britain – Gordon Walker – Île Amsterdam.

**1977-79:** WINTER-OVER

*DAMIEN II* – France – Jérôme & Sally Poncet.

1977-78: South Georgia, South Shetlands, Antarctic Peninsula.

1978: WINTERED at Avian Island, Antarctic Peninsula.

1978 -79: Antarctic Peninsula, South Shetlands, South Georgia, Falkland Islands, Tierra del Fuego.

Poncet, S. 1982. *Le Grand Hiver.* Editions Arthaud.

**1977-78:**

*SOLO* – Australia – David Lewis and crew – Macquarie Island, Balleny Islands, Cape

Adare region in Ross Sea.

Lewis, D. 1979. *Voyage To The Ice.* Australian Broadcasting Commission and William Collins Sons & Co Ltd.

## 1978-79:

*CAMEO* – New Zealand – Lionel Jefcoate and crew – Auckland Island.

*CHAMPI* – France – Jacques Peignon – Tierra del Fuego, Antarctic Peninsula, South Shetlands, South Georgia.

Peignon, J. 1980. April issue of French *Neptune Nautisme* magazine.

*ISATIS* – France – Jean & Claudine Lescure and 1 crew – Antipodes Island, Antarctic Peninsula, Palmer Station, South Shetlands, Tierra del Fuego.

Lescure, C. 1980. March and November issues of French *Neptune Nautisme* magazine.

*KOTICK* – France -Oleg Bely & Sophie Labruhe – South Georgia.

Labruhe, S. 1980. January issue of French *Neptune Nautisme* magazine.

*WILLIWAW* – Belgium – Willy de Roos and 1 crew – Tierra del Fuego, South Shetlands, Antarctic Peninsula.

De Roos, W. 1985. Inaccessible Horizon. Editions Arthaud.

## 1979-80:

*BASILE* – France – Bertrand Dubois and crew – South Georgia (Mt. Paget), Gough Island.

Dubois, B. 1980. *Les Montagnes de l'Ocean.* Editions du Pen Duick.

Film: *Où Va-Tu Basile?*

*MOMO* – France – Charles Ferchaud and Jean-Marie Ferchaud – South Georgia, Antarctic Peninsula, South Shetlands, South Orkneys, Gough Island.

## 1980-82: WINTER OVER

*KIM* – France – Michel Chopard, Daniel Gazanion, Bruno Maroux and Claude Monchaud.

1980-81: South Shetlands, Antarctic Peninsula

1981: WINTERED at Petermann Island, Antarctic Peninsula.

1981-82: Antarctic Peninsula, South Shetlands, South Georgia.

Chopard, M., Gazanion, D., Maroux, B. and Monchaud, C. 1983. *Kim: Mer, Soleil, Glaces.* Editions Pen Duick.

Maroux, B., Monchaud, C., Chopard, M., and Gazanion, D. 1983. *Kim: Images de Mer, Soleil, Glace.* Editions Pen Duick.

Film: *KIM.*

## 1980-81:

*DELPHINE* – France – Henri & Megan Goiot – Îles St Paul and Amsterdam

*DIONE* – Britain – Brian Harrison and crew – Tierra del Fuego, South Shetlands, Antarctic Peninsula.

Harrison, B. July 1981 issue of British *SAIL* magazine.

*ISATIS II* – France – Jean & Claudine Lescure – Antarctic Peninsula, South Shetlands, Falkland Islands.

*SHIELDAIG* – France – Yves Beulac and crew – South Georgia.

## 1981-82:

*CAIMAN* – Panama – Igor Raggio and crew – South Georgia.

*CINQ GARS POUR-* France – Olivier Gouon and crew – South Georgia.

Video footage.

*DICK SMITH EXPLORER* – Australia – David Lewis and crew – Commonwealth Bay area and George V Land, and Dumont D'Urville station in Terre Adélie.

*ENDEAVOUR* – Panama – Patrick Cudennec and crew – Îles Kerguelen.

*FREYDIS* – Germany – Erich & Heide Wilts and crew – Falkland Islands, South Shetlands, Antarctic Peninsula, Tierra del Fuego.
Wilts, H. 1983. *Weit im Norden Liegt Kap Hoorn.* Delius Klasing.

*ISATIS II* – France – Jean & Claudine Leścure – Falkland Islands, South Georgia.

*MAZEPPA* – France – Yannick Trancart and 1 crew – Îles Kerguelen, Saint-Paul, Amsterdam.
Trancart, Y. 1985. *Au-Dela Des Tempetes.* Presses de la Cite.

*QUAKSTER* – Australia – Karl & Diane Freeman – Falkland Islands, South Georgia.

*33-EXPORT-* France – Thomas Phillippe and A. Schaff – Îles Kerguelen.

### 1982-84:

*DICK SMITH EXPLORER-* Australia – David Lewis, Don Richards and crew.
1982-83: Rauer Islands on Ingrid Christensen Coast, and Île Amsterdam.
1983: WINTERED at Rauer Islands in Prydz Bay.
1983-84: Rauer Islands, Davis Station, and Mirny Station area.
Lewis, D. and George, M. 1987. *Icebound in Antarctica.* Secker & Warburg.
Chester, J. Going to Extremes

### 1982-83:

*ANACONDA II* – Australia – Josko Grubic (skipper), William Blunt, Ross Vining and crew – Heard Island.
Film: *Land of Wind, Ice and Fire.*
*CHEYNES II* – Australia – Heard Island.
*DAMIEN II* – France – Jérôme & Sally Poncet

and family and crew – Antarctic Peninsula, South Shetlands, Falkland Islands.

*GRAHAM* – France – Philippe Cardis and crew – Falkland Islands, Tierra del Fuego, South Shetlands, Antarctic Peninsula, South Georgia.
Cardis, P. and Franco, M. 1984. *Terre de Graham.* Editions Arthaud.
Film: Graham.

*WILLIWAW* – Belgium – Willy de Roos and 1 crew -Tierra del Fuego, South Shetlands, Antarctic Peninsula.
De Roos, W. 1985. *Inaccessible Horizon.* Editions Arthaud.
Film: ?

### 1983-84:

*DAMIEN II* – France – Jérôme & Sally Poncet and family – Falkland Islands, South Georgia, South Orkneys, South Shetlands, Antarctic Peninsula.

*F'MURR* – France – Jean-Jacques Argoud, Arnaud de Buron and Patrick Cloatre – Falkland Islands, South Shetlands, Antarctic Peninsula, South Georgia.

*MAZEPPA-* France – Yannick Trancart and Jo Adami – Tierra del Fuego, Antarctic Peninsula, South Shetlands, Falkland Islands.
Trancart, Y. 1985. *Au-Dela Des Tempetes.* Presses de la Cite.

*NORTHERN LIGHT* – Sweden – Rolf Bjelke & Deborah Shapiro – Tierra del Fuego, Antarctic Peninsula, South Shetlands, Falkland Islands.
Bjelke, R. and Shapiro, D. 1986. *Northern Light.* Macdonald Queene Anne Press.

*KOALA* – France – A. Pasqualini and crew – South Georgia.

*WAYFARER IV* – New Zealand – Mark Hammond and crew – Macquarie, Snares, Campbell and Auckland Islands.

**1984:**

*TOTORORE* – New Zealand – Gerry Clark and crew – Tierra del Fuego, Falkland Islands, South Georgia in winter.
Clark, G. 1988. *The Totorore Voyage.* Century Hutchinson Ltd.

**1984-85:**

*BASILE* – France – Alain Caradec and crew – Tierra del Fuego, South Shetlands, Antarctic Peninsula,
Morosini, M. 1985. *Antarctica '85' Expedition Report.*
Film: *Vers le Sud.* Swiss/Italian TV.
*DICK SMITH EXPLORER* – Australia – Don Richards (skipper), William Blunt, Ross Vining and crew – Cape Denison in George V Land, and Dumont D'Urville Station in Terre Adélie.
Chester, J. 1985. *Going To Extremes.* Doubleday.
*DIEL* – South Africa – Bernhard Diebold and crew – Antarctic Peninsula, South Shetlands.
*KOTICK* – France – Oleg Bely & Sophie Labruhe – Falkland Islands, South Shetlands, Antarctic Peninsula, Tierra del Fuego.
*KSAR* – France – Jean-Paul Bassaget and 1 crew – Falkland Islands, Tierra del Fuego, South Shetlands, Antarctic Peninsula.
*MARARA* – France – ? and ? crew – Île St. Paul.
*SUNDOWNER* – Germany – Volker Matten & Randy ? – Falkland Islands, Tierra del Fuego, South Shetlands, Antarctic Peninsula.
*TANERA* – France – Christophe Constans – Île St. Paul.
*TOTORORE* – New Zealand – Gerry Clark and crew -Tierra del Fuego, South Georgia, Antarctic Peninsula, South Shetlands.
Clark, G. 1988. *The Totorore Voyage.* Century Hutchinson Ltd.

**1985:**

*TOTORORE* – New Zealand – Gerry Clark, Julia von Meyer, and Chris Sale – Tierra del Fuego, South Georgia, South Sandwich Islands, Bouvetoya in winter.
Clark, G. 1988. *The Totorore Voyage.* Century Hutchinson Ltd.

**1985-86:**

*AOMI* – Japan – Yoshi – Tierra del Fuego, South Shetlands, Antarctic Peninsula.
*BELLE-ETOILE* – France – Jephig (Jean-Joseph) Terrier and crew – Antarctic Peninsula, South Shetlands, Tierra del Fuego.
*COCORLI* – France – Olivier Troalen & Ketty Cavrois – South Shetlands, Antarctic Peninsula, Falkland Islands, Tierra del Fuego.
*DAMIEN II* – France – Jérôme & Sally Poncet and family and crew – Falkland Islands, South Georgia, South Shetlands, Antarctic Peninsula.
Osborne, B. 1987. January issue of British *Yacht World* magazine.
*JACRIS* – Italy – Francesco Bastion – Île St. Paul.
*JAMO* – France – Jacques & Monique Auvray – Îles St. Paul and Crozet.
*KOTICK* – France – Oleg Bely & Sophie Labruhe – Tierra del Fuego, South Shetlands, Antarctic Peninsula.
*PALAWAN* – USA – Thomas Watson and crew – Antarctic Peninsula, South Shetlands.
*RAPA NUI* – France – Patrick & Gaby Jourdan and 1 crew – Falkland Islands, South Georgia, South Shetlands, Antarctic Peninsula, Tierra del Fuego.
Klink, A. 1986. May issue of Brazilian *Afinal* magazine.
*RIQUITA* – Australia – Barry Lewis and crew – Cape Adare region and Cape Hallett in the Ross Sea.

*SKUA* – France – Frédéric André and crew – South Georgia.

*TOTORORE* – New Zealand – Gerry Clark – Marion and Prince Edward Islands, Îles Crozet and Kerguelen, Heard and McDonald Islands.
Clark, G. 1986. *The Totorore Voyage.* Century Hutchinson Ltd.

**1986-87:**

*ANNE* – USA – William Reid Stowe and crew – South Shetlands, Antarctic Peninsula, Deception Island, Port Lockroy, Palmer Station, Falkland Islands.

*ANTARES* – France – Georges & Michelle Meffre and crew – Île St. Paul.
Meffre, G. & M. 1992. *Les Vagabonds de l'Ocean.* LN Editions.

*DAMIEN II* – France – Jérôme & Sally Poncet and crew – Falkland Islands, South Georgia, Antarctic Peninsula, South Orkneys.

*JAMO* – France – Jacques & Monique Auvray – Île St. Paul.

*KOTICK* – France – Oleg Bely & Sophie Labruhe, and crew – Tierra del Fuego, South Shetlands, Antarctic Peninsula.

*LEISURELY LEO* – Britain – ? – South Georgia.

*MATA HIVA* – France – Patrick Leclerq and crew – Tierra del Fuego, South Shetlands, Antarctic Peninsula.

*NORTHANGER* – Britain – Rick Thomas and crew – Antarctic Peninsula, South Shetlands, Falkland Islands.
Tierney, M. 1987. *Australian Geographic* magazine.

*WARBABY* – Bermuda – Warren Brown and crew – Falkland Islands, South Shetlands, Antarctic Peninsula, Tierra del Fuego.

Gore-Grimes, J. 1987. *Irish Cruising Club Report.*

Newbold Smith, E. 1987. *Antarctic, Chile, Falklands Islands, Graham Land.* In RCC Journal 1987. Roving Commissions Ltd.

**1987-88:**

*ALLAN & VI THISTLETHWAYTE* (ex *DICK SMITH EXPLORER*) – Australia – Don Richards (skipper), Greg Mortimer and 9 crew – Cape Hallett in Ross Sea area, Mt. Minto.
Hall, L. and Chester, J. 1988. *The Loneliest Mountain.* Simon & Schuster.

*DAMIEN II* – France – Jérôme & Sally Poncet and crew – Falkland Islands, South Georgia.
Poncet, S. 1988. April issue of *National Geographic* magazine.

*KOTICK* – France – Oleg Bely & Sophie Labruhe and crew – Tierra del Fuego, South Shetlands, Antarctic Peninsula, Falkland Islands.

*NOUANNI* – France – Patrick & Dominique Feron and 4 crew – Tierra del Fuego, South Shetlands, Antarctic Peninsula, Falkland Islands.

*PELAGIC* – Britain – Skip Novak and crew – Antarctic Peninsula, South Shetlands, South Georgia.
Novak, S. 1987. No. 45 issue of American magazine *Nautical Quarterly.*
Novak. S. 1989, January issue of American magazine *Yachting.*
Film: *No Problem Pelagic.* Iceberg Films and RTSI. Swiss/Italian TV.

*PEQUOD* – Argentina – Hernon Alvarez Forn and crew – Tierra del Fuego, South Shetlands.

*SEA TOMATO* – USA – Edward Gilette and Mark Eisenbach – Tierra del Fuego, South Shetlands.

Gilette, E. 1988. January issue of *National Geographic* magazine.

**1988-89:**

*AMRIA* – France – Jean Chambe and crew – Antarctic Peninsula, South Shetlands.

*CLOUD NINE-* USA – Roger Swanson and crew – Antarctic Peninsula, South Shetlands. Swanson, R. 1989. American *Cruising World* magazine.

*CROIX SAINT-PAUL* – France – Alex Foucard and crew – Tierra del Fuego, South Shetlands, Antarctic Peninsula.

*DAMIEN II* – France – Jérôme Poncet and crew – Falkland Islands, South Shetlands, Antarctic Peninsula.

*HERACLITUS* – USA – Klaus Elberle and crew – Tierra del Fuego, South Shetlands, Antarctic Peninsula, Falkland Islands.

*KOTICK* – France – Alain Caradec and crew – Tierra del Fuego, South Shetlands, Antarctic Peninsula.

*SCHERZO* – France – Pascal Grinberg & Françoise de la Bernadie – Falkland Islands, South Shetlands, Antarctic Peninsula, Tierra del Fuego.

*TRADE WIND* – New Zealand – Mark Hammond and crew – Macquarie, Campbell and Auckland Islands.

**1989-90:**

*CYGANA* – USA – Charles ? and wife and crew – Tierra del Fuego, Antarctic Peninsula.

*DAMIEN II* – France – Jérôme & Sally Poncet and crew – Falkland Islands, South Shetlands, Antarctic Peninsula.

Janichon, G. 1990. May and June issues of French *Voiles et Voiliers* magazine.

Film: *Antarctic Wildlife Adventure*. National Geographic.

*DURACELL* – USA – Mike Plant – Campbell Island.

*JANTINE* – Holland – Dick & Helle Koopmans – Falkland Islands, Tierra del Fuego, South Shetlands, Antarctic Peninsula.

*KOTICK* – France – Alain Caradec & Claudine Brouazin and crew – Tierra del Fuego, South Shetlands, Antarctic Peninsula: two cruises.

*SATURNIN* – France – Christophe Houdaille and Patrick Fradin – Falkland Islands, South Georgia, Bouvet, Marion and Heard islands, Îles Crozet and Kerguelen.

*SCHERZO* – France – Pascal Grinberg and 1 crew – Falkland Islands, Tierra del Fuego, South Shetlands, Antarctic Peninsula.

*SKOOKUM* – Canada – Geoff Payne & Margaret Hough – Falkland Islands, South Shetlands, Antarctic Peninsula.

SOL – Australia – Chris Elliot (skipper), Tracey Brown and crew – Tierra del Fuego, South Shetlands, Antarctic Peninsula.

Film: *Journey To The Bottom Of The World*. National Geographic.

*TAO* – Germany – ? and crew – Tierra del Fuego, South Shetlands.

*THEOROS* – Switzerland – Eric Barde and 1 crew – Tierra del Fuego, Antarctic Peninsula, Falkland Islands.

TRADEWIND – New Zealand – Mark Hammond and crew – Campbell, Auckland and Macquarie islands.

*UAP ANTARCTICA* – France – Jean Collet and crew – Tierra del Fuego, South Shetlands, Antarctic Peninsula, South Orkneys, Peter Øy Island, Macquarie Island.

**1989-91:** WINTER-OVERS

*OVIRI* – France – Hugues Delignières.
1989-90: Tierra del Fuego, Antarctic Peninsula.
1990: WINTERED at Hovgaard Island, Antarctic
Peninsula.
1990-91: Antarctic Peninsula, Tierra del Fuego.
Delignières, H. 1990. May issue of French
*Neptune Yachting* magazine.
Delignières, H. 1991. December issue of French
*Voiles et Voiliers* magazine.

*PARATI* – Brazil – Amyr Klink.
1989-90: South Shetlands, Antarctic Peninsula.
1990: WINTERED at Wiencke Island, Antarctic
Peninsula.
1990-91: Antarctic Peninsula.

**1990-92:** WINTER-OVERS

*FREYDIS* – Germany – Erich & Heidi Wilts and
crew.
1990-91: Falkland Islands, Tierra del Fuego,
South Shetlands, Antarctic Peninsula.
1991: WINTERED at Deception Island, South
Shetlands – Erich and Heidi Wilts.
1991-92: South Shetlands, Tierra del Fuego.
Wilts, H. 1992. Sternstunden auf allen Ozeanen.
Wilts, H. 1992. Gerstrandet in der Weissen Holle.
*NORTHERN LIGHT* – Sweden – Rolf Bjelke &
Deborah Shapiro.
1990-91: Tierra del Fuego, South Shetlands,
Antarctic Peninsula.
1991: WINTERED at Hovgaard Island, Antarctic
Peninsula.
1991-92: Antarctic Peninsula.
Shapiro, D. Time on Ice.
*SATURNIN* – France – Christophe Houdaille
1990-91: South Georgia.
1991: WINTERED at South Georgia.
1991-92: South Georgia, Falkland Islands.

**1990-91:**

*BALTAZAR* – France – Bertrand Dubois and
crew – Tierra del Fuego, South Shetlands,
Antarctic Peninsula.
*CAROUSEL* – France – ? – Macquarie Island.
*CROIX SAINT-PAUL* – France – Alex Foucard
and crew – Tierra del Fuego, South Shetlands,
Antarctic Peninsula.
*CROUSTET* –– France – Bernard Espinet
– Macquarie Island
*DAMIEN II* – Falkland Islands – Jérôme Poncet
and crew – Falkland Islands, South Georgia.
*DIEL* – South Africa – Bernhard Diebold and
crew – South Georgia.
*FAREWELL* – Fabien Poncet and crew
– Falkland Islands, South Georgia
*KEKILISTRION* – France – Olivier Pauffin and
crew – Tierra del Fuego, Antarctic Peninsula.
*KOTICK* – France – Alain Caradec & Claudine
Brouazin and crew – Tierra del Fuego, South
Georgia.
Allisy, D. 1991. December issue of French
*Voiles et Voiliers* magazine.
*KOTIC II* – Brazil – Oleg Bely & Sophie
Labruhe and crew – Terra del Fuego, South
Shetlands, Antarctic Peninsula – two cruises.
*PASSAGE* – France – Jean-Pierre Danjean and
crew – Tierra del Fuego, Antarctic Peninsula.
*PELAGIC* – Britain – Skip Novak and crew
– Tierra del Fuego, South Shetlands, Antarctic
Peninsula.
Novak, S. 1991 Various sailing magazines.
Film: various for British TV.
*RAPA NUI* – Brazil – Hernan Atila and crew
– South Shetlands, Antarctic Peninsula.
*RED SUN* – Japan – Tatesumu Kidokoro
– Falkland Islands, South Shetlands, Antarctic
Peninsula, Tierra del Fuego.
*SANTA MARIA* – Germany – Wolf & Melanie

Kloss – Tierra del Fuego, Antarctic Peninsula.

*SOL* – Australia – Keith Clement and crew – Tierra del Fuego, Falkland Islands, South Georgia.

*SORGENFRI* – Norway – Peder Krogh and Johann Pedersen – Falkland Islands, South Shetlands, Antarctic Peninsula, Tierra del Fuego.

*TRADE WIND* – New Zealand – Mark Hammond and crew – Auckland, Campbell and Snares islands.

### 1991-92:

*ANTARCTICA (ex UAP ANTARCTICA)* – France – Jean Collet (skipper), Jean-Louis Etienne and crew – Falkland Islands, Tierra del Fuego, South Shetlands, Antarctic Peninsula, South Orkneys, South Georgia, Weddell Sea.

Le Corre, Yvon. 1992. *Antarctide*. Gallimard.

Etienne, J-L. et de Marliave C. 1992. *Antarctica: une aventure dans les mers australes*. Gallimard.

*ASMA* – Germany – Clark Stede & Michelle Poncini- Tierra del Fuego, Antarctic Peninsula.

*ASSENT* – Britain – William Kerr and 1 crew – Falkland Islands, Antarctic Peninsula, South Shetlands.

Ker, W. and Ormerod, L. 1992. *Beyond Neptune's Bellows* in "Royal Cruising Club journal" 1992. Roving Commissions Ltd.

*BALTAZAR* – France – Bertrand Dubois & Siv Follin and crew – Tierra del Fuego, South Shetlands, Antarctic Peninsula.

*BETELGEUSE* – USA – Sue-Anne Colding and crew – Tierra del Fuego, Antarctic Peninsula, South Georgia.

*BORA UNIVERSAL* – New Zealand – John Martin and crew – Gough Island.

*C FLAT SCHERZO* – France – Pascal &

Adrienne Grinberg and crew – South Georgia.

*CLOUD NINE* – USA – Roger Swanson and crew – Tierra del Fuego, Antarctic Peninsula.

*CROIX SAINT-PAUL* – France – Alex Foucard and crew – Tierra del Fuego, South Shetlands, Antarctic Peninsula.

*CURLEW* – Britain – Tim & Pauline Carr – Tierra del Fuego, Falkland Islands, South Shetlands, Antarctic Peninsula.

Carr, T. and P. 1992. "Last Port of Call" in American magazine *Classic Boat* Nov 92

Carr, T. and P. 1993. "Catching the Tide" in British magazine *Yachting Monthly*, June 93

*DAMIEN II* – Falkland Islands – Jérôme Poncet and crew – Falkland Islands, South Shetland Islands, Antarctic Peninsula, Weddell Sea.

*DIEL* – South Africa – Bernhard Diebold and crew – South Georgia.

*DUMMER SUMMER* – New Zealand – Capt. Bond and crew – Gough Island.

*KOTICK* – France – Alain Caradec & Claudine Brouazin and crew – Tierra del Fuego, South Shetlands, Antarctic Peninsula. Two cruises.

*KOTIC II* – Brazil – Oleg Bely and Sophie Labruhe and crew – Tierra del Fuego, Antarctic Peninsula. .

*MERIVUKKO* – Finland – Pertti Duwcker and Mani Suanto – Antarctic Peninsula.

*PELAGIC* – Britain – Skip Novak & Julia Crossley and crew – Tierra del Fuego, South Shetlands, Antarctic Peninsula.

Novak, S. 1992. In British magazine *Yachting World*, Vol. 144 No 4009, September 1992

*POLARKA* – Czechoslovakia – Rudolf Krautschneider – Marion Island, Heard Island, Île Crozet, Île Kerguelen.

*SATURNIN* – France – Christophe Houdaille – South Georgia, Falkland Islands.

*SKOOKUM* – Australia – Geoff Payne &

Margaret Hough and crew – Falkland Islands, South Georgia.
Payne, G. 1994. "Skookum's South Atlantic Finale" in American magazine *Cruising World* Dec 94.
*TEAKE HADEWYCH* – Netherlands – Eerde Beulakker & Hedwig van den Brink and crew – Tierra del Fuego, Falkland Islands, South Shetlands, Antarctic Peninsula, South Georgia.
Beulakker, E. 1994. Naar Koude Kusten.
*THEOROS* – Switzerland – Eric Barde – Tierra del Fuego, South Georgia, Falkland Islands.
*TRADEWIND* – New Zealand – Mark Hammond and crew – Tierra del Fuego, Antarctic Peninsula, Falkland Islands, South Georgia, South Shetlands.

**1992-93:**
*BUTTERCUP* – Australia – Donald McIntyre and crew – Commonwealth Bay.
*CROIX SAINT-PAUL II* – France – Alex & Marie-Blanche Foucard and crew – Tierra del Fuego, South Shetlands, Antarctic Peninsula.
*CURLEW* – Britain – Tim & Pauline Carr – Falkland Islands, South Georgia. WINTERED in South Georgia 1993.
Carr, P. 1992 "Letter from the Carrs" in American magazine *Cruising Club News* CCA Dec 94.
Carr, T. and P. 1993. "Privilege" in American magazine CCA *Cruising Club News* Dec 93.
*DAHU* – Switzerland –
*DAMIEN II* – Falkland Islands – Jérôme & Sally Poncet and crew – Falkland Islands, South Georgia.
*DIVA* – France – Didier & Gaelle Forest and I crew – Tierra del Fuego, Falkland Islands, South Georgia, South Orkneys, South Shetlands, Antarctic Peninsula.

*FREYDIS* – Germany -- Erich & Heidi Wilts and crew – Falkland Islands, South Georgia, South Sandwich Islands.
*INIQUITY* – Australia – John Hendly and crew – Commonwealth Bay, Balleny Islands, Macquarie Island.
*JANTINE* – Holland – Dick & Helle Koopmans – Îles Kerguelen.
*KEKILISTRION* – France – Olivier Pauffin de Saint-Morel and crew – Tierra del Fuego, Antarctic Peninsula, South Shetlands.
*KOTIC II* – Brazil – Oleg Bely & Sophie Labruhe and crew – Tierra del Fuego, Antarctic Peninsula.
*KOTICK* – France – Alain Caradec & Claudine Brouazin and crew – Tierra del Fuego, Falkland Islands, South Georgia, Antarctic Peninsula.
*MARI STELLA* – France – Christine Darde and Jacqueline Darde – Tierra del Fuego, Falkland Islands, South Georgia.
*MORITZ D* – Germany – Harald & Hedel Voss – Tierra del Fuego, Falkland Islands, South Shetlands, Antarctic Peninsula.
*OVIRI* – France – Hugues Delignières & Marie-Paul Guillaumot – Tierra del Fuego, Falkland Islands, South Shetlands, Antarctic Peninsula.
*PEGGOTTY* – New Zealand – Alan & Barbara Sendall & family – South Shetlands, Falkland Islands.
*PELAGIC* – British Virgin Islands – Skip Novak and crew – Tierra del Fuego, South Shetlands, Antarctic Peninsula.
POLARKA – Czechoslovakia – Rudolf Krautschneider and crew – South Shetlands, Falkland Islands.

**1993-94:**
*ANDROMEDA* – Germany – Joachim Scheid & wife)- South Georgia.

*ANTARCTICA* – France – Jean Collet (skipper), Jean-Louis Etienne (owner) and crew – Ross Island, Ross Sea.

*CALLAS* – Argentina – Jorge Trabuchi and crew – Tierra del Fuego, South Shetlands, Antarctic Peninsula.

*CHANSON DE LECQ* – Great Britain – Josephine Hunter and 1 crew – Falkland Islands, South Georgia.

Hunter, J. 1994. in South African yachting magazine.

*CROIX SAINT-PAUL II* – France – Alex & Marie-Blanche Foucard and crew – Tierra del Fuego, Antarctic Peninsula.

*CURLEW* – Great Britain – Tim & Pauline Carr – South Georgia. WINTERED at South Georgia 1994.

Carr, T. and P. 1994. "Antarctic Legacy" in British magazine *Classic Boat* Jan 94.

Carr, T. and P. 1994. "Antarctic Graveyard" in British magazine *Classic Boat* Feb 94.

Carr, T. and P. 1994. "In Shackleton's Wake" in British magazine *Yachting Monthly* Jan94.

Carr, T, and P. 1994. "Test of Time and Tide" in American magazine *Wooden Boat* Sep 94.

Carr, T. and P. 1994. "The Magic Still Exists" in American magazine *SAIL* Sep 94.

Carr, T. and P. 1994. "Down Easter, Down South" in American magazine *Maine Boats and Harbours* Dec 94.

*DAMIEN II* – Falkland Islands – Jérôme & Sally Poncet and crew – Tierra del Fuego, Falkland Islands, South Shetlands, Antarctic Peninsula, South Georgia

*DODO'S DELIGHT* – Great Britain – Robert Shepton and crew – Falkland Islands, South Shetlands, Antarctic Peninsula.

*EVOHE* – New Zealand – Steven Kafka and crew – Campbell Island.

*FREYDIS* – Germany – Erich & Heide Wilts and crew – Indian Ocean.

*KEKILISTRION* – France – Olivier Pauffin and crew – Tierra del Fuego, Antarctic Peninsula, South Shetlands.

*LOCO LOLA* – Switzerland – Jean Nydegger and crew – Tierra del Fuego, Antarctic Peninsula.

*METAPASSION* – Australia – Georges & Michele Meffre – Tierra del Fuego, Falkland Islands, South Shetlands, Antarctic Peninsula.

*MORITZ D* – Germany – Harald & Hedel Voss – Falkland Islands, South Georgia, Tierra del Fuego.

*PELAGIC* – British Virgin Islands – Skip Novak & Julia Crossley and crew – Tierra del Fuego, South Shetlands, Antarctic Peninsula.

*POPAYE* – France – Olivier & Agnès Gouon and crew – South Georgia, Falkland Islands, South Orkneys, Tierra del Fuego.

*SHINGEBISS II* – USA – Lawrence & Maxine Bailey and I crew – Falkland Islands, South Shetlands.

Bailey, L. 1994. in American magazine CCA *Cruising Club News* Vol XXXVII No. I.

*TOTORORE* – New Zealand – Gerry Clark and crew – Antipodes Island.

*WAR BABY* – USA – Warren Brown and crew – Snares, Auckland and Campbell Islands.

WILD FLOWER – Australia – Anne-Lise Guy – South Georgia.

**1994- 96:** WINTER OVER
*SATURNIN* – France – Christophe Houdaille – Îles Kerguelen. WINTERED at L'Anse Aldebert, Îles Kerguelen 1995.

Houdaille, C. 1999. Au Vent Des Kerguelens. Editions Transboreal.

**1994-1995:**

*BADGER* – Great Britain – Peter & Annie Hill – Falkland Islands, South Georgia, South Orkneys, Gough Island.

*BEAGLE START II* – Great Britain – James Leonard and crew – Tierra del Fuego, South Shetland Islands, Antarctic Peninsula.

*BLUE LINE* (?) – ? and crew – Antarctic Peninsula, Tierra del Fuego, South Georgia.

*CHANSON DE LECQ* – Great Britain – Josephine Hunter – Île St Paul. Hunter, J. 1995 "Dismasted" in British magazine *Yachting Monthly* Dec 95.

*CROIX SAINT-PAUL II* – France – Alex Foucard and crew – Tierra del Fuego, Antarctic Peninsula.

*CHRYSALIDE* – France – Benoit Rouault and crew – Tierra del Fuego, Antarctic Peninsula.

CURLEW – Britain – Tim & Pauline Carr (2)- South Georgia. WINTERED at South Georgia 1995.
Carr, T. and P. 1995. "Best of Both Worlds" in British magazine *Yachting World* Jan 95.
Carr, T. and P. 1995. "Ocean Harbour" in American magazine *SAIL* March 95.
Carr, T. and P. 1995. "Albatross" in British magazine *Yachting World*.
Carr, T. and P. 1995. "Antarctic Outpost" in British magazine *Yachting Monthly*.

*DAMIEN II* – Falkland Islands – Jérôme & Sally Poncet and crew – Falkland Islands, South Georgia.

*ECUREUIL-POITOU-CHARENTES II* – France – Isabelle Autissier – Îles Kerguelen.

*ENGLISH ROSE VI* – Great Britain – John & Marie-Christine Ridgeway and crew – Tierra del Fuego, Antarctic Peninsula, South Shetlands, South Georgia.

*FERNANDE* – France – Pascal & Adrienne Grinberg and crew – Tierra del Fuego, Antarctic Peninsula, South Shetlands.

*FLEUR AUSTRALE* – France – Philippe Poupon & Christine Merlet – Falkland Islands, Antarctic Peninsula, South Shetland Islands.

*IAORANA* – Belgium – Marcel Petter and crew – Antarctic Peninsula, South Shetlands, Tierra del Fuego.

*ITASCA* – Cayman Islands – Allan Jouning and crew – Antarctic Peninsula, South Shetlands, Tierra del Fuego.

*JUPITER* – Great Britain – Roberto Migiaccio and crew – South Georgia, Tierra del Fuego.

*KEKILISTRION* – France – Olivier Pauffin de Saint-Morel and crew – Tierra del Fuego, South Shetlands, Antarctic Peninsula.

*KOTICK* – France – Alain Caradec & Claudine Brouazin and crew – Antarctic Peninsula, South Shetlands, Tierra del Fuego.

*KOTIC II* – Brazil – Oleg Bely and Sophie Labruhe and crew – South Georgia, Tierra del Fuego.

*METAPASSION* – Australia – Georges & Michelle Meffre and crew – Tierra del Fuego, South Shetlands, Antarctic Peninsula.

*METOLIUS* – USA – Kim & Reidun Lungren and crew – Falkland Islands, Tierra del Fuego, Antarctic Peninsula.

*PELAGIC* – British Virgin Islands – Skip Novak and crew – Antarctic Peninsula.

*PACÔME III* (ex *ESPRIT D'ÉQUIPE*)– France – Rémy de Vivie and crew – Tierra del Fuego, South Shetlands

*SANTA MARIA* – Germany – Wolfgang Kloss and crew – Tierra del Fuego, Antarctic Peninsula.

*SATURNIN* – France – Christophe Houdaille – Île Kerguelen (WINTERED OVER 1995)

*SHINGEBISS II* – USA – Larry & Maxine Bailey

– Falkland Islands, South Georgia.

*SPIRIT OF SYDNEY* – Australia – Stephen Corrigan and crew – Commonwealth Bay, East Antarctica.

*TOTORORE* – New Zealand – Gerry Clark and crew – Antipodes Island, Campbell Island.

*WESTRI* – USA – Christopher West and crew – Antarctic Peninsula.

**1995-1996:**

*CROIX SAINT-PAUL II* – France – Alex Foucard and crew – Tierra del Fuego, Falkland Islands, South Georgia, South Shetlands, Antarctic Peninsula.

*DAMIEN II* – Falkland Islands – Jérôme Poncet and crew – Falkland Islands, South Georgia.

*FERNANDE* – France – Pascal & Adrienne Grinberg and crew – Tierra del Fuego, Falkland Islands, South Georgia.

*FLEUR AUSTRALE* – France – Philippe Poupon & Christine Merlet – Falkland Islands, South Georgia.

*FREYA* – Netherlands – Wilhelmus Hofstede and crew – Tierra del Fuego, Antarctic Peninsula.

*FREYDIS* – Germany – Erich and Heide Wilts and crew – Macquarie Island, Scott Island, Campbell Island.

*GALLAD II* – France – Yves Bouyx and crew – Tierra del Fuego, South Shetlands, Antarctic Peninsula.

*HETAIROS* – Germany – Brent Dow (Skipper), Otto Happel (owner) and crew – Tierra del Fuego, Antarctic Peninsula.

*JENNY VON WESTPHALEN* – Germany – Von Schmeling and crew – Tierra del Fuego, Antarctic Peninsula

*KEKILISTRION* – France – Olivier Pauffin

de Saint-Morel – Tierra del Fuego, South Shetlands, Antarctic Peninsula.

*KOTICK* – France – Alain Caradec & Claudine Brouazin and crew – Tierra del Fuego, South Shetlands, Antarctic Peninsula.

*KOTIC II* – Brazil – Oleg Bely and Sophie Labruhe and crew – Tierra del Fuego, South Shetlands, Antarctic Peninsula.

*MAHINA TIARE* – USA – John Neal and crew – Tierra del Fuego, South Shetlands, Antarctic Peninsula.

*NORTHANGER* – New Zealand – Greg Landreth & Keri Pashuk – Tierra del Fuego, South Shetlands, Antarctic Peninsula.

*PASSE PARTOUT* – British Virgin Islands – Cornelius Ackerman and crew – Tierra del FuegoAntarctic Peninsula.

*PELAGIC* – Great Britain – Skip Novak and crew – Tierra del Fuego, South Shetlands, Antarctic Peninsula.

*SANTA MARIA* – Germany – Wolfgang Kloss and crew – Tierra del Fuego, South Shetlands, Antarctic Peninsula.

*SARAH W. VORWERK* – Germany – Henk Boersma and crew – Tierra del Fuego, South Shetlands, Antarctic Peninsula.

*SPIRIT OF SYDNEY* – Australia – Stephen Corrigan and crew – Commonwealth Bay, East Antarctica.

*ST. MICHEL* – Germany – Joachim Campe and crew – Tierra del Fuego, South Shetlands, Antarctic Peninsula.

*TENERA LUNA* – Italy – Paolo Mascheroni and crew- Tierra del Fuego, South Shetlands, Antarctic Peninsula.

*TOTORORE* – New Zealand – Gerry Clark and crew – Auckland Island.

*WARBABY* – Bermuda – Warren Brown and crew – Campbell Island, Auckland Island.

*WILD FLOWER* – Australia – ? and crew
– South Georgia.
*YARRA* – Switzerland – Eric Bretscher and
crew – Tierra del Fuego, Antarctic Peninsula.

**1996 -1997:**
*ADIX* – Spain – Paul Goss and crew – Antarctic
Peninsula.
*AYESHA* – Great Britain – Miles Quitmann and
crew – Antarctic Peninsula.
*C-LISE II-* USA – Gordon Schmidt and crew
– Antarctic Peninsula.
*CROUSTAT* – France – Bernard Espinet
– Tierra del Fuego, Falkland Islands, South
Georgia, Îles Kerguelen.
*CROIX SAINT-PAUL II* – France – Alex Foucard
and crew – Tierra del Fuego, South Shetlands,
Antarctic Peninsula.
*DAMIEN II* – Falkland Islands – Jérôme Poncet
and crew – Falkland Islands, South Georgia,
South Sandwich Islands.
*FERNANDE* – France – Pascal & Adrienne
Grinberg and crew – Tierra del Fuego,
Antarctic Peninsula.
*GOLDEN FLEECE* – Falkland Islands – Eef
Willems and crew – Tierra del Fuego, South
Shetlands, South Georgia, Falkland Islands,
Antarctic Peninsula.
*HRVATSKA CIGRA* – Croatia – Mladen Sutej
and crew – Antarctic Peninsula.
*KEKILISTRION* – France – Olivier Pauffin
de Saint-Morel – Tierra del Fuego, South
Shetlands, Antarctic Peninsula.
*KOTICK* – France – Alain Caradec & Claudine
Brouazin and crew – Tierra del Fuego, South
Shetlands, Antarctic Peninsula.
*KOTIC II* – Brazil – Oleg Bely & Sophie
Labruhe and crew – Tierra del Fuego, South
Shetlands, Antarctic Peninsula.

*LE BOULARD* – France – Jean Monzo and crew
– Tierra del Fuego, South Shetlands, Antarctic
Peninsula.
*NORTHANGER* – New Zealand – Greg
Landreth & Keri Pashuk – Tierra del Fuego,
South Shetlands, Antarctic Peninsula.
*ONRUST II* – Australia – Dirk Tober and crew
– Antarctic Peninsula.
*PELAGIC* – Great Britain – Skip Novak and
crew – Tierra del Fuego, South Shetlands,
South Georgia.
*POLAR MIST* – USA – Richard Crowe and crew
– Antarctic Peninsula.
*RAEL* – Spain – Bubi Sanso and crew
– Antarctic Peninsula.
*SANTA MARIA* – Germany – Wolfgang Kloss
and crew – Tierra del Fuego, South Shetlands,
Antarctic Peninsula.
*SARAH W. VORWERK* – Germany – Henk
Boersma and crew – Tierra del Fuego, South
Shetlands, South Georgia, Antarctic Peninsula.
*TAONUI* – Canada – Tony & Corinne Gooch
– Antarctic Peninsula.
*TOM CREAN* – Irish Republic – Frank Nugent
and crew – South Shetland Islands.
*VAGUE-A-BOND* – France – Claude & Liliane
Veniard – Tierra del Fuego, South Shetlands,
Antarctic Peninsula.
*VALHALLA* – France – Pascale Boimard and
crew – Tierra del Fuego, South Shetlands,
Antarctic Peninsula.

**1997-1998:**
*ARDEVORE OF ROSELAND* – Great Britain
– Tim & Sofia Hugh-Trafford – South Georgia,
Falkland Islands.
*BALTAZAR* – France – Bertrand Dubois & Siv
Follin – Tierra del Fuego, South Shetlands,
Antarctic Peninsula.

*CROIX SAINT-PAUL II* – France – Alex Foucard and crew – Tierra del Fuego, South Shetland Islands, Antarctic Peninsula.

*DENEB OF RYE* – Great Britain – Hugues Delignieres and crew – Tierra del Fuego, South Shetlands, Antarctic Peninsula.

*DON VITO* – Argentina – Claudio Casolari and crew – South Shetland Islands, Antarctic Peninsula.

*FERNANDE* – France – Pascal & Adrienne Grinberg and crew – Tierra del Fuego, South Shetlands, Antarctic Peninsula.

*FREYDIS* – Germany – Erich & Heide Wilts – South Shetland Islands, Antarctic Peninsula.

*GOLDEN FLEECE* – Falkland Islands – Jérôme Poncet and crew – Falkland Islands, South Sandwich Islands.

*IF* – France – Hugues Delignieres & Marie-Paul Guillaumot and crew – Tierra del Fuego, Falkland Islands, South Georgia.

*ITASCA* – Cayman Islands – Allan Jouning and crew – Tierra del Fuego, South Shetland Islands, Antarctic Peninsula.

*KEKILISTRION* – France – Olivier Pauffin de Saint-Morel – Tierra del Fuego, South Shetland Islands.

*KOTICK* – France – Alain Caradec & Claudine Brouazin – Falkland Islands, South Georgia, Tierra del Fuego, Antarctic Peninsula.

*KOTIC II* – France – Oleg Bely & Sophie Labruhe – Tierra del Fuego, South Shetland Islands Antarctic Peninsula.

*LE BOULARD* – France – Jean Monzo and crew – Tierra del Fuego, South Shetland Islands Antarctic Peninsula.

*MORITZ D* – Germany – Harald & Hedel Voss – South Georgia. WINTERED OVER 1998.

*NAJAT* – Australia – Elisabeth Post and crew – Tierra del Fuego, South Shetland Islands Antarctic Peninsula.

*OOSTERSCHELDE* – Netherlands – Dick van Andel and crew – Tierra del Fuego, South Shetland Islands Antarctic Peninsula.

*PARMELIA* – Australia – Roger Wallis and crew – Tierra del Fuego, South Shetland Islands Antarctic Peninsula.

*PELAGIC* – British Virgin Islands – Skip Novak, Hamish Laird and crew – Tierra del Fuego, South Shetland Islands Antarctic Peninsula.

*PEN DUICK III* – France – Patrick Tabarly and crew – Tierra del Fuego, South Shetland Islands Antarctic Peninsula.

*PHILOS* – Swizerland – Eric Barde and crew – Tierra del Fuego, South Shetland Islands Antarctic Peninsula.

*SANTA MARIA* – Germany – Wolfgang Kloss and crew – Tierra del Fuego, South Shetland Islands Antarctic Peninsula.

*SARAH W. VORWERK* – Germany – Henk Boersma and crew – Tierra del Fuego, South Shetland Islands Antarctic Peninsula.

*SPOSMOKER II* – Netherlands – Julio Verstaeten and crew – Tierra del Fuego, South Shetland Islands Antarctic Peninsula.

*TIGRE MOU* – France – Hervé & Béatrice Legoff and crew – Tierra del Fuego, South Georgia.

*VALHALLA* – France – Pascal Boimard and crew – Tierra del Fuego, South Shetland Islands Antarctic Peninsula.

**1998-1999:**

*AVENTURA III* – Great Britain – James Cornell and crew – Tierra del Fuego, South Shetland Islands Antarctic Peninsula

*BALTAZAR* – France – Bertrand Dubois & Siv Follin and crew – Tierra del Fuego, South Shetland Islands Antarctic Peninsula.

*BESERK* – Norway – Jarle Andhoy and crew – Tierra del Fuego, South Shetland Islands Antarctic Peninsula.

*CROIX SAINT-PAUL II* – France – Alex Foucard and crew – Tierra del Fuego, South Georgia, South Shetland Islands, Antarctic Peninsula.

*EXCESS* – Australia – Terry Travers and crew

*FERNANDE* – France – Pascal Grinberg and crew – Tierra del Fuego, South Shetland Islands Antarctic Peninsula.

*FIONA* – USA – Eric Forsyth and crew – Tierra del Fuego, South Shetland Islands Antarctic Peninsula.

*FUTURO* – Germany – Christopher Harding and crew – Tierra del Fuego, South Shetland Islands Antarctic Peninsula.

*GOLDEN FLEECE* – Falkland Islands – Jérôme Poncet and crew – Tierra del Fuego, Falkland Islands, Antarctic Peninsula.

*IRONBARK* – Australia – Trevor Robertson – Antarctic Peninsula. WINTERED OVER 1999 at Port Lockroy.

*KOTIC II* – Brazil – Oleg Bely & Sophie Labruhe and crew – Tierra del Fuego, South Georgia, South Shetland Islands, Antarctic Peninsula.

*LE BOULARD* – France – Jean Monzo and crew – Tierra del Fuego, Antarctic Peninsula.

*MEANDER* – Netherlands – Eef Willems and crew – Tierra del Fuego, Antarctic Peninsula.

*MERITSH LOUISE* – British Virgin Islands – Skip Novak and crew – Tierra del Fuego, Antarctic Peninsula.

*MORITZ D* – Germany – Harald & Hedel Voss – South Georgia, WINTERED OVER 1999.

*OOSTERSCHELDE* – Netherlands – Dick van Andel and crew – Tierra del Fuego, South Georgia, South Shetland Islands, Antarctic Peninsula.

*PARATI* – Brazil – Amyr Klink – South Georgia, circumnavigated Antarctica.

*PELAGIC* – Great Britain – Hamish Laird and crew – Tierra del Fuego, South Georgia, South Shetland Islands, Antarctic Peninsula.

*PHILOS* – Switzerland – Eric Barde and crew – Tierra del Fuego, Antarctic Peninsula.

*REGAIN* – France – Vincent Malquit – South Georgia, Antarctic Peninsula.

*RISQUE* – USA – Lou Morgan and crew – Tierra del Fuego, Antarctic Peninsula.

*SANTA MARIA* – Germany – Wolfgang Kloss and crew – Tierra del Fuego, Antarctic Peninsula.

*SARAH W. VORWERK* – Germany – Henk Boersma and crew – Tierra del Fuego, Antarctic Peninsula.

*TAONUI* – Canada – Tony & Corinne Gooch –South Georgia

*TOTORORE* – New Zealand – Gerry Clark and crew – Tierra del Fuego, Antipodes Island.

*VIENS-TU?* – France – Claude Plee and crew – Tierra del Fuego, South Shetland Islands, Antarctic Peninsula.

*VOYOU* – Austria – Claude Appaldo and crew – Tierra del Fuego, Antarctic Peninsula.

*WANDERER III* – Denmark – Thies & Kiki Matzen – South Georgia, Tierra del Fuego, Antarctic Peninsula.

### 1999-2000:

*2041* – Great Britain – Mark Hopkins and crew – Tierra del Fuego, Antarctic Peninsula.

*ALDERMAN* – Great Britain – James Wakeford and crew – Tierra del Fuego, Antarctic Peninsula.

*ARKA* – France – Didier Laut and crew – Tierra del Fuego, Antarctic Peninsula.

ANNEX VIII: SOUTHERN OCEAN YACHT VOYAGES

*AVENTURA* – Great Britain – James Cornell and crew – Tierra del Fuego, Antarctic Peninsula.
*BALTAZAR* – France – Bertrand Dubois & Siv Follin and crew – France – Tierra del Fuego, Antarctic Peninsula.
*BESERK* – Norway – Jarle Andhoy and crew – Tierra del Fuego, Antarctic Peninsula.
*BLUE NORTHERN* – USA – Wayne Harden and crew – Tierra del Fuego, Antarctic Peninsula.
*CALLIBISTRIS* – France – Michel & Jacqueline Hennebert – Falkland Islands, South Georgia Tierra del Fuego.
*CROIX SAINT-PAUL II* – France – Julio Brunet and crew – Tierra del Fuego, Falkland Islands, South Georgia, South Shetland Islands, Antarctic Peninsula.
*DAGMAR AAEN* – Germany – Martin Friedrichs, Arved Fuchs and crew – South Shetland Islands, South Georgia.
*EXPRESS CRUSADER* – Great Britain – Richard Corbet and crew – Tierra del Fuego, Antarctic Peninsula.
*FLEUR AUSTRALE* – France – Philippe Poupon & Christine Merlet and crew – Falkland Islands, South Georgia.
GOLDEN FLEECE – Falkland Islands – Jérôme Poncet and crew – Falklands Islands, South Georgia, South Shetland Islands, Antarctic Peninsula.
*JAMES CAIRD II* – Germany – Arved Fuchs and crew – South Shetlands, South Georgia.
*KOTIC II* – Brazil – Oleg Bely & Sophie Labruhe and crew – Tierra del Fuego, South Georgia, South Shetland Islands, Antarctic Peninsula.
*KOTICK* – France – Alain & Claudine Caradec and crew – Tierra del Fuego, South Georgia, South Shetland Islands, Antarctic Peninsula.

*L'AVENTURE* – France – Christian Galard and crew – Tierra del Fuego, Antarctic Peninsula.
*MEANDER* – Netherlands – Eef Willems and crew – Tierra del Fuego, Antarctic Peninsula.
*MORITZ D* – Germany – Harald & Hedel Voss – South Georgia, Falkland Islands.
*OOSTERSCHELDE* – Netherlands – Dick van Andel and crew – Tierra del Fuego, South Shetland Islands, Antarctic Peninsula.
*PELAGIC* – British Virgin Islands – Hamish Laird and crew – Tierra del Fuego, Antarctic Peninsula.
*PHILOS* – Switzerland – Eric Barde and crew – Tierra del Fuego, Antarctic Peninsula.
*SANTA MARIA* – Germany – Wolfgang Kloss and crew – Tierra del Fuego, Antarctic Peninsula.
*SARAH. W. VORWERK* – Germany – Henk Boersma and crew – Tierra del Fuego, South Georgia, South Shetland Islands, Antarctic Peninsula.
*SAVANNAH* – France – Joel & Dominique Marc – South Georgia, South Shetland Islands, Antarctic Peninsula.
*SHANTOOTI* – Great Britain – Richard Hayworth and crew – Tierra del Fuego, Antarctic Peninsula.
*THE DOVE* – Great Britain – Larry Tyler and crew – Tierra del Fuego, Antarctic Peninsula.
TIAMA – New Zealand – Henk & Bunny Haazen and crew – Tierra del Fuego, Antarctic Peninsula.
TOOLUKA – Australia – Roger Wallis and crew – Tierra del Fuego, South Georgia, South Shetland Islands, Antarctic Peninsula.

# Acronyms and abbreviations

| | |
|---|---|
| **AAD** | Australian Antarctic Division |
| **ADD** | Antarctic Digital Database |
| **ASMA** | Antarctic Specially Managed Area |
| **ASPA** | Antarctic Specially Protected Area |
| **ATCM** | Antarctic Treaty Consultative Meeting |
| **ATS** | Antarctic Treaty System |
| **BAS** | British Antarctic Survey |
| **CCAMLR** | Convention on the Conservation of Antarctic Marine Living Resources |
| **CEE** | Comprehensive Environmental Evaluation |
| **CEP** | Committee for Environmental Protection |
| **COMNAP** | Council of Managers of National Antarctic Programs |
| **EIA** | Environmental Impact Assessment |
| **FCO** | Foreign and Commonwealth Office |
| **FIG** | Falkland Islands Government |
| **GPS** | Global Positioning System |
| **GSGSSI** | Government of South Georgia and the South Sandwich Islands |
| **Hbr** | Harbour |
| **HSM** | Historic Site and Monument |
| **IAATO** | International Association of Antarctica Tour Operators |
| **IEE** | Initial Environmental Evaluation |
| **IMO** | International Maritime Organization |
| **LTER** | Long Term Ecological Research (Program) |
| **MARPOL** | International Convention for the Prevention of Pollution from Ships |
| **nm** | nautical mile |
| **NSF** | National Science Foundation (US) |
| **SAR** | Search and Rescue |
| **SCAR** | Scientific Committee on Antarctic Research |
| **SOLAS** | International Convention for the Safety of Life at Sea |
| **SPA** | Specially Protected Area |
| **SPRI** | Scott Polar Research Institute |
| **SSSI** | Site of Special Scientific Interest |
| **TAAF** | Terres Australes et Antarctiques Françaises |
| **USAP** | United States Antarctic Program |